W9-AQF-734

GREENLAND

ICELAND

ARCTIC CIRCLE

NORWAY

SWEDEN

FINLAND

SOVIET UNION

LABRADOR

SENECA

EUROPE

ATLANTIC

OCEAN

EROKEE

OCEAN

INOLE

DESERT

AFRICA

VENEZUELA

COLOMBIA

Congo River

EQUATOR

OR

Amazon River

INDIAN

SOUTH AMERICA

OCEAN

PERU

BRAZIL

KALAHARI

PARAGUAY

GRAPHIC 70

African Pygmies

Lapps

Ainus (Hokkaido, Japan)

Australian Aborigines

People
in
Twilight

BY ADRIEN STOUTENBURG

A VANISHING THUNDER:
Extinct and Threatened American Birds

ANIMALS AT BAY:
Rare and Rescued American Wildlife

PEOPLE IN TWILIGHT:
Vanishing and Changing Cultures

People in Twilight

Vanishing and Changing Cultures

by
Adrien Stoutenburg

Illustrated with photographs

DOUBLEDAY & COMPANY, INC.
Garden City, New York

Acknowledgements

To Joan Davlin, of the Department of Anthropology at San Francisco State College, my special thanks for her expert help in correcting errors of fact or interpretation in the manuscript of this book. If any errors remain, the responsibility is wholly mine.

I also wish to thank Dr. Charles J. Keim of the University of Alaska for the time he granted me at the very beginning of this project. I am indebted, too, to Kay J. Kennedy of Wien Consolidated Airlines, who cooperated with photographs and other materials; to Mayo Murry of the *Daily News-Miner,* Fairbanks, and to Howard Rock, editor of the *Tundra Times.* This list would be by no means complete without mention of my friend and hostess Norma Martin, of College, Alaska, who through her offices at the university there, provided the opportunity for me to interview these individuals and others, including Alaskan natives themselves.

A.S.

Contents

Preface

An airplane swoops low over a South American jungle. Below, dark-skinned natives scurry from their mud huts or leap from their fish traps, seizing bows and arrows to shoot at the great, noisy "bird" soaring above the trees. The arrows, even though poison-tipped, fall harmlessly to earth, but the monstrous, winged shape departs and the warriors believe they have frightened it away. Above, the photographer in the airplane feels triumph, having caught the scene on his camera film.

Thousands of miles westward, across the Pacific Ocean, a group of naked, brown-skinned people follow drifting smoke signals across the Australian desert, trudging toward a small tent in the distance. They are a broad-nosed people with deep-set eyes under heavy eye ridges. In the lead, the men carry spears or boomerangs, while women and children follow with digging sticks. They are on their way to see the strange, foreign English woman Kabbarli, Grandmother, who will give them white man's flour and rice since they are hungry, having failed to find sufficient roots, berries, or lizards to eat.

Far above the Arctic Circle at the northernmost point of the United States, a group of Alaskan Eskimos and a white man are hunting whales from boats along the edge of an ice floe. The white man is new to the treeless land of Point Barrow and new to whaling. Just when the natives begin to grin slyly at his clumsy white man's way of hunting, he harpoons a white beluga whale.

The Eskimos help him haul the struggling catch onto the ice, and the white hunter is eager to kill it at once. No, no, the Eskimos warn. He must wait. Native women in fur-lined parkas hurry forward with a bucket of fresh water. This they pour carefully into the blow hole of the whale, and slosh the rest over its head. The dying whale, they explain, must have a drink of something fresh before being cut up; otherwise its spirit will tell the rest of the whales that it was mistreated and no more whales will ever permit themselves to be taken.

In the South Seas, natives of New Guinea watch closely as warships anchor off shore. Japanese soldiers land, bringing remarkable machines with them—some with iron treads that move like mechanical snails, others with metal snouts that plow through the thickest trees. Other machines haul loads of cargo that include strange, small boxes from which voices can be heard by turning a knob. There are wires, poles, canvas, steel knives, ingenious weapons.

Then there is the booming of great guns, bombs hurtling down from the clouds, and more ships coming. The men with a yellow cast to their skin retreat as Americans or Australians take over. The new, pale-complexioned soldiers bring still more remarkable cargo in their mighty ships, or drop it on land from powerful birds of the air.

The natives compare the possessions of the strangers with their own. Theirs seem now not so clever as they had thought, and they desire the invaders' machines and tools for themselves. They will wait. Someday the invaders will die, they think, or disappear. A great ship will come over the horizon, bearing a cargo meant especially for *them!* They watch on the beaches, day and night. They chant, make sacrifices, and dance around sacred fires.

Back in the land where the American soldiers come from, the Hopi Indians of the Southwest hold their rain dance, going through rituals that are meant to wring moisture from the dry, hot sky. There the priests of the Snake Society perform age-old dance patterns which culminate in the priests taking living snakes in their mouths. Swaying to the beat of drums and rhythmical chants, the dancer holds the middle of the snake's body in his teeth so that the creature's head is free to move. Tourists crowd around to watch while Indian vendors peddle pop, gum, and souvenirs.

Some of these things happened in the near past. Some, such as the Snake Dance, or the ritual dances of Eskimos or Hawaiians, continue but they are increasingly performances put on as tourist attractions, their ancient meanings forgotten even by those who perform them, though some of the very old may recall the beauty and spiritual significance that was once so important to the ceremonies. Even among the younger generation, old ways and beliefs cling in spite of the impact of modern technology and the pressures of the dominant, white man's culture.

Only ten years before the United States astronauts first stepped onto the moon, a seventeen-year-old Navaho boy was tending a flock of sheep near the tiny reservation community of Indian Wells, Arizona. It was a hot, humid day. Gray and white thunderclouds rolled up from the mesas and canyons and rumbled over a small cluster of buildings that included a United States post office. Beyond the town, widely separated dots in an empty landscape, stood Navaho hogans. Some were ordinary frame shacks, a number having television aerials on their roofs. Others were older buildings, six-sided enclosures of logs with circular domes resembling beehives, smoke hole openings in the center.

The sheep that the boy Harry Joe was tending were thin creatures, their fleece as raveled as the wind and sun-beaten land where only the toughest grasses and shrubs grow, and where only equally enduring people can survive on the acres allotted to them. With each rumble of thunder, the sheep started nervously. Harry Joe felt uneasy too. One of the sayings of the older people was "Never laugh aloud in the face of a storm." There were many such sayings having to do with untrustworthy spirits and ghosts, part of the Navaho beliefs that had been handed down through centuries of time. The beliefs persisted in spite of the Christian missions, television, radios, and comic strips.

It was superstition, said the younger Navahos, denying earlier beliefs as a result of exposure to other influences while working in the cities or serving in the military forces. Still, many of them spoke more with an air of defiance than conviction.

A lightning bolt crashed near and Harry Joe ducked toward a wagon abandoned in a swatch of sagebrush. Just as he reached it, another bolt drilled downward, killing him instantly.

When Harry Joe did not return to his hogan, his elderly parents set out to search for him. They found his body under the wagon but in spite of their grief they did not dare to go near it. To do so, they believed, or even to touch anything that had been struck by lightning—a stone, a tree, a stick—meant that they could go blind or suffer some other terrible consequence. Dead bodies, under any circumstances, were feared, but this one doubly so.

In desperation, they sent a message to the town asking the native police to come and remove their son's body for burial. But the Navaho police were as fearful as they and refused. That night, the mourning relatives built a brush fire about fifty yards from the body and stood watching over it.

At dawn, the parents still remained, helpless to know how to deal with the problem. They wanted a Christian burial for their son, for the missionaries who lived among them had convinced them that this was proper. But in order to have this, Harry Joe must be moved into town to the mission house.

Finally, they drove their truck to town and beseeched the postmaster, Herbert S. Hukriede, for help. Hukriede was a white man who had spent twelve years on the reservation and had coped with such problems before. He drove his own truck to the lightning-scorched spot, took Harry Joe's body to the mission, bought new clothes for the dead youth, and picked out a coffin.

On July 17, 1959, the missionary conducted the services at an Indian burial ground. Hukriede dropped the young man's saddle, his lariat, a few pieces of cheap jewelry, and an empty suitcase into the grave. From a distance, the dead boy's family watched the ceremony. A month later, Hukriede was given an award for public service above and beyond the call of duty by the Assistant Postmaster General.

A newspaper report quoted Hukriede as saying, "I don't feel so deserving. Other white men have done the same kind of thing. Maybe some day we'll dispel the superstition."

Much more than "superstition" is involved in the behavior of people whose ancestors belong to societies that existed and flourished long before white explorers discovered them. Whether Eskimo, Indian, Bushman, or Australian Aborigine, each group developed beliefs and customs in order to cope with the challenges of environment—whether desert or forest or frigid north—and to the mysteries of the universe. Though these peoples had no so-called scientific knowledge of why winds blow, or why the moon goes through its different phases, they learned to work and live with nature, as they had to in order to survive. Without understanding the exact physical laws involved in the effect of the moon's pull upon the tides, still they knew how the tides acted and how to utilize the ebb and flow for their own purposes in sailing or fishing; or how to find the least sign of water in seemingly featureless sand, the wariest movement of an animal in the jungle. They were very aware of the various patterns of natural forces, and the interrelatedness of all things—what modern man has belatedly recognized and calls ecology. And they lived with respect for, and obedience to, the laws of the natural world, which was their true home.

Surrounding and permeating the natural world was the supernatural, and spirits that could inhabit not only living creatures but rocks, forests, and rivers. The "soul" of a tree was not just a figure of speech for them, but an actual presence. Spirit beings were everywhere—in the whale, the volcano, the sun. Some spirits were easily displeased. If a famine occurred, perhaps the goddess of the corn—or of the bison or salmon—had not been treated with proper respect. Not to treat the highest forces with respect was to risk punishment or death. Such peoples would be no more apt to defy the supernatural or the immediate spirit world than a devout Christian would shake his fist at Heaven or desecrate the Cross. As we have our religious symbols, they had theirs.

Like people everywhere, these early societies struggled with the question of how the world and man were created. Natives of the Gilbert Islands believed man was generated from the sparks and ashes of a divinely ignited tree. Hawaiians thought the gods simply spat on the ground to form human beings. Winnebago Indians believed that their creator-god, Earthmaker, formed human beings out of the earth—a conception that has a striking similarity to the Old Testament version of the creation of Adam.

It was essential to keep in favor with the supernatural beings or the ghosts of the dead. Each culture developed certain rites that must be followed—specific ceremonies, ordeals, offerings, dances—in order to placate the ruling powers. Magic was also used to try to attain desirable ends. Certain rites combined both religious and social significance. Boys and men had to perform specific ceremonies that would make them powerful hunters or warriors. Young girls had to go through detailed rites that would make them function well as wives and mothers. If the strict rituals were violated, death or destruction could follow from the displeasure of the gods.

Most powerful among such societies were the shamans, witch doctors, or medicine men, who were believed to have direct access to the supernatural and so could control not only crops and weather and the hunt, but life and death. The sacred symbols of the group were in their keeping, and it was they who presided over the important ceremonies. The communal wisdom, the laws and legends of a tribe or clan were passed on from one generation to another over many centuries. Although a few small, non-Western societies operated at a crude level with the most rudimentary tools and crafts, several others achieved technical skills that remain a marvel today.

Long before Europeans ever came to the shores of South or North America, the Mayas of Yucatan developed a calendar and a numerical system comparable to our own calendar and arithmetic. Further, they conceived the abstract quantity of zero, one of the outstanding achievements of the human intellect, and this was over two thousand years ago. They were also excellent engineers and masons, building dams, reservoirs, great pyramids, and cities.

The ancient Aztecs were master builders, too; their capital city standing where Mexico City is today. The Spanish invaders of 1519 were astonished at their first sight of the splendid temples, canals, and pyramids such "savages" had built. They felt amazement again when they found in Peru the marvelous highway of the Incas spiraling three thousand miles across the Andes, the complex irrigation systems and terraced fields. And in the North American Southwest, they found remarkable cliff dwellings, abandoned by the early architects who designed them.

Before and after the Spanish were other explorers—Italian, Portuguese, French, Dutch, English—sailing their fragile ships to new worlds in search of gold, spices, colonies, trade. Wherever they landed they brought their own religions, customs, and goods, all of which were strange to the indigenous peoples of the lands they visited. To most of the explorers the natives seemed brutish, ignorant, and pagan. They were considered barbarians to be killed or used as slaves; representatives of the Church hoped to redeem them through conversion to Christianity. Some visitors had praise, one of these being an early colonizer under Sir Walter Raleigh in Virginia. Describing his reception in an American Indian village in 1584, he wrote, "We were entertained with all love and kindness, and with as much bounty (after their manner) as they could possibly devise. We found the people most gentle, loving, and faithful, void of all guile and treason, and such as live after the manner of the Golden Age."

The name "Indian" for the original inhabitants of the Americas has created much confusion. The problem started with Columbus who believed that he had reached the Indies (India) when he touched land in the Bahamas, and so called the inhabitants Indians. Other names have been suggested—Amerindian, Native American, First Americans, or Tribal Americans. But "Indian" remains the most usual name. The term "red man" is in disrepute, and has no accuracy, anyhow, any more than do the labels "white" or "yellow" or "black." No skin colors, in spite of the current term "black is beautiful," are that distinct. Skin hues vary among individuals of any group, and the term "race" is one that has an increasingly loose definition, even to being described simply as a group which has lived in a certain place for a certain length of time. Many ethnologists, anthropologists who specialize in a study of early cultures and changes especially among technologically primitive groups, consider that there are only three primary divisions, the Caucasian (loosely, white race), Negroid (loosely, black race), and Mongoloid (loosely, yellow race), each with various subdivisions. But the term race has been so misused and misapplied that it has been largely replaced in scientific studies by the term "ethnic stock" or "group."

Most of the knowledge we have of earlier peoples is the product of observations made by members of the Western world and are consequently heavily weighted in favor of Western culture. There was no question in the minds of explorers, missionaries, and traders but that their beliefs and ways were far superior to those of the natives they encountered, many of whom they considered non-human. This feeling of superiority is not confined to the white man. It is common for people to feel that the members of their own society—nation, clan, tribe, or even political party—are superior to others. The Lapps of Scandinavia reserve the term "human being" for themselves only, while the Cherokee Indians call themselves the "principal people." Greenland Eskimos say, "Europeans visit us to learn good manners," and the Hottentot proclaims, "We are the men of men." This is called ethnocentrism, and certainly Americans have long boasted of their superiority over all other peoples.

The story of how whites dispossessed the American Indians of their land and their way of life is a familiar one, a story still unfinished. With superior weapons and a long background of almost unremitting warfare, the first Europeans on our shores proceeded to force themselves and their beliefs on the native Americans. In America, as in Australia, New Guinea, or Africa—wherever there is a primitive or semiprimitive native population suddenly introduced to a newer technology and alien attitudes—there is a culture clash, the weaker forced to retreat before the stronger. Not that conquest is always the result of firepower or sharper swords. For many native societies, alien disease germs turned out to be the real conqueror. Smallpox and syphilis killed untold numbers of natives who had never been exposed to them before. Even before the Pilgrims landed at Plymouth Rock, an estimated

90 per cent of the Indians in the region had already died of smallpox, introduced earlier by other Europeans.

Only in the most remote pockets of the world are there peoples still untouched by modern civilization, and it is just a matter of time before they, too, will feel the impact of the bulldozer, the air strip, the oil pipeline, and the computer. They, like the indigenous groups being rapidly swallowed into the mainly white culture, or destroyed by it, will be forced to surrender most of their old way of life.

The early Aztecs, the Cliff Dwellers, the Mandan Indians, to mention only a few civilizations, have already vanished. Today, many other native tribes and cultures are vanishing, or changing to such a degree that it may be said they have vanished. They have little choice. They must become "acculturated" to the prevailing culture, learn to adjust to it, and master the social and technical skills required, or they perish. Yet, many are highly resistant to sacrificing their traditions and spiritual ties. Among those who do want to become "Americanized" or "Australianized" the barriers of poverty, lack of education, and racial discrimination stand in their way. Too often there is patronage on one side, active hostility or despair on the other.

One of the United States' and other dominant nations' major challenges is how to provide means for earlier cultures to perpetuate their ancient heritages, encouraging them at the same time to contribute their talents to the mainstream of society if they so desire. Some of the customs of premodern cultures were— or are—cruel to our eyes: human sacrifice, self-mutilation, bloody initiation rites—as cruel as many of our customs have seemed to them. Yet, many past cultures had a vision of the world and of nature that contained a basic wisdom and a reverence for life that modern societies often lack, as is evident in "civilized" man's widespread destruction of the natural environment and widespread wars.

If the Indian's religious regard for the earth, the Congo Pygmy's love of the forest could be combined with present-day technology in the use and conservation of such resources, surely all would benefit. No one can live completely as he wishes. In a city, all automobile drivers, whether American or Yapese, must stop for traffic signals. But it would seem that we could live alongside each other with respect for each other's attitudes and aspirations, each contributing the special value that is his, prizing the very richness of such diversity.

People
in
Twilight

1.
Prairie, Plain, Forest, and Desert

INDIANS OF NORTH AMERICA

The July sun was warm on the buffalo grass and the huts of the Wichita Indians. Across what is now Kansas, a troop of men came riding forward, Spanish soldiers under the command of Francisco Coronado. Guided by a captive Pawnee Indian who had told the Spaniards of a place called Quivira where everything was made of gold, Coronado and his conquistadores looked expectantly across the rippling plains.

The Wichita, staring from the shadows of their grass shelters, had never seen horses before and it seemed to them that rider and mount were all one creature. The gleaming armor seemed a part of the whole beast, and though the faces above the gleam seemed human-looking they were sickly pale. The lower part of the creature had four slim legs, blowing neck hair, and large round nostrils. The only animals the Great Plains Indians had managed to put to their service were dogs. These carried heavy packs strapped to their backs or were hitched to travois, two light poles that dragged behind the animals like a crude sled laden with baggage.

As for Coronado, he stared in dismay at the drab Indian camp, the scrawny dogs, the ashes of fires sprinkled with scraps of bone and other debris. A year before, in 1540, he had set out from Mexico in search of a fabled kingdom, the Seven Cities of Cibola to the north. And though he had reached Cibola—the Zuñi country of New Mexico—he had found no gleaming gold or wealth in the Indian pueblos there. Now, after spending the winter among Pueblo Indians near present-day Santa Fe, he was again faced with nothing but seemingly empty land and skulking, hungry savages. In fury, he ordered his men to strangle the Pawnee guide, then wheeled his horse around and led the soldiers back toward the Rio Grande country they had left after killing so many of the natives that the once thriving pueblos there were now empty.

Such was the Wichita Indians' first experience with the Spanish and with horses. Though they did not know it, their ancient forebears had been familiar with the ancestor of the horse, a small, wild creature that had existed during the Pleistocene period, or Ice Age. That original wild horse was now extinct, as were the mammoth, the giant sloth, the prehistoric giant beaver, the saber-toothed tiger. Long gone, too, were the first

Indians who had slowly crossed to America from Asia, over a land bridge that then stretched across the Bering Strait, perhaps following grazing mammoths. It was a process of centuries, seemingly an unwitting migration. With the most primitive of tools, these wandering hunters of Mongoloid stock (which includes the Chinese, Tibetans, Malays, Eskimos, Turks, and Finns) moved across the central plain of Alaska, then ventured onward, generation after generation, finding new hunting and fishing grounds.

Centuries before the arrival of Columbus, their few but scattered numbers stretched from coast to coast, from the frozen tundra of the north to the hot deserts, from mountain to plain, from inland swamp to the rumbling seashore. Each group had its special way of life, depending on the environment and on the group's particular development. Some tribes were roving hunters. Some tended to remain in one spot, planting crops to increase their food supply. Some were basket makers, some wove on hand looms; some were potters, though none knew the use of the wheel. Different groups spoke different languages, with many varied dialects within one language. War, as we know it, was relatively rare, though there were tribal battles. The red man (so called because he often painted his brownish skin with reddish earth hues) survived in general harmony with the natural world.

Less than one hundred years after Coronado's visit to the Wichita, the Plains Indians themselves had horses, descendants of lost or captured Spanish herds. Although they called the animals "big dogs," having no name for horses, and at first ate them before learning to ride them, horses changed the Plains Indians' way of existence. On horseback, the Indian hunter could travel far in search of bison and other game, and the horse could carry much more than could dogs or squaws. Around 1750, the horses from the Southwest and traders' guns from the Northeast met on the plains. So it was that the Plains Indians' culture developed and flourished, to become the stereotype in Western movies and wild West stories. From these came the popular conception of Indians as primarily warriors—fast-riding redskins in feathered war bonnets attacking wagon trains, fiendishly murdering and torturing "peaceful" whites.

Well before that, with the very beginnings of white settlement on the eastern seaboard, the European colonists had met Indians of a different kind. Although these Indians of New England hunted, fished, and trapped, they also engaged in agriculture. One of the Indians' greatest gifts to the colonists and to the present-day world was corn. It was Indian corn, together with beans, potatoes, and squash, that helped to save the starving Pilgrims who founded New Plymouth after the landing of the *Mayflower* in 1620. "A special instrument of God," was how the Pilgrim leader William Bradford spoke of an Indian who taught these English settlers the way to plant corn and nourish it by putting dead fish in the corn hills for fertilizer.

There, in Massachusetts, peace continued between the white man and Indian for more than ten years. Still, it was an uneasy peace for both English and Dutch were pressing into lands that belonged to the Indians. One native group in particular was being crushed by the westward push, the Pequot Indians of the Connecticut River Valley. They took up arms to resist, with the result that the Dutch and English joined together, approached their silent wigwams at dawn, set the wigwams afire, and riddled the fleeing natives with musket shot. A leading Puritan clergyman, Cotton Mather, was delighted with the massacre for he considered Indians "the veriest ruins of mankind."

A religious group called Quakers and the early French, who came to trade instead of take over the land, tried to keep the peace and deal justly with the Indians. But even the best-meaning had little or no understanding of Indian ways. Land ownership was very important to white settlers. Indians could not conceive of claiming private ownership to land, asserting only use rights. Hospitality was a part of Indian tradition and no stranger was ever denied food or shelter. When whites took advantage of this traditional hospitality, the Indian could not understand. He felt more bewildered than belligerent. When the English and French armies shot at each other in an attempt to kill as many contestants as possible, he was again confused. It took a long while for him to realize that his very being, physical and spiritual, was crucially threatened and to start active resistance. It was not that he was either patient or a "slow learner." It was simply that he lived by his own rules, markedly different in most aspects from those of the invaders. At the time Jamestown, Virginia, was settled in 1607, Chief Powhatan could have struck the tiny colony a devastating blow, but he did not. By the time he died, so many white settlers had moved in that it was too late for the Indians to reclaim what they had lost.

The same story was repeated elsewhere. Like Powhatan, other Indians waited to strike back until it was too late. And certain tribes wasted their strength fighting each other. European traders and settlers took advantage of tribal conflicts for their own purposes. French, English, and Dutch fought each other for land and trade, and Indian allies fought with them. Few Indian groups could afford to maintain a standing army, and such wars as they had among themselves were seldom for conquest. Often an attacking side, believing that nothing was worth having its members killed would stop fighting after having suffered casualties. Certain groups abhorred warfare in any form, particularly the Hopi of the Southwest, among the most peaceful people on earth. But when it became essential for the Indians of the Northeast, or the Plains, or the Northwest to fight for their land and lives, they did, valiantly and long.

Here and there, certain far-seeing Indian leaders realized the need for the outnumbered and divided Indians to band together to resist the steady encroachment of whites. These leaders who struggled to unify their kinsmen against a common enemy left their names emblazoned on Indian history, the true patriots of their people. The name of the Ottawa chief Pontiac means much more than the make of a recent American model of car, as the name of the Apache warrior Geronimo is more than a modern battle cry.

The briefest history of such chiefs shows how year by year Indians were pushed back ever westward from the vanishing wilderness. First, it was the New England Indians who failed under "King" Philip, a Wampanoag leader in the war of 1675–76. Philip was among the first to try to rally the tribes together in a common cause, and came close to defeating the colonists. Then, with the help of an Indian informer, Philip was killed. The remaining bands were wiped out, one by one, bringing an end to Indian power in New England.

In the area between Lake Erie and Lake Ontario, Pontiac led what has been called Pontiac's Rebellion against the English. Although he ravaged the frontier, capturing almost every English position in the West except Pittsburgh and Detroit, he eventually surrendered to superior white forces and to division among his followers, in 1765.

Still, some hope of an Indian nation remained. It was Tecumseh who made one of the last stands to create a sovereign Indian kingdom in the midst of encircling white men. Although he was a Shawnee he considered himself an Indian first. And he was inspired by the Americans who had successfully fought their own revolution against the British king. Surely, Tecumseh thought, those Americans would realize the Indian need for freedom and independence. Some did, but a majority did not. Caught in the complexities of the War of 1812 between the young United States and Great Britain, he was doomed; with his death in a final battle in the fall of 1813, his dream of an Indian nation died with him.

Onward came the white legions: soldiers, trappers, missionaries, farmers. Black Hawk, warrior of the Sauk, tried to stem the tide. Born where the city of Rock Island, Illinois, stands today, he, too, worked to band the tribes together, appealing to those as far away as Texas. Defeated, forced to sign a humiliating treaty in 1831, Black Hawk fought back again, but with diminishing forces. Final defeat came in a battle at the Mississippi River, forty miles above present Prairie du Chien, and the aging chief was taken prisoner. In 1836, the artist George Catlin saw him and described him as a "poor dethroned monarch. With an old frock coat and brown hat on, and a cane in his hand, he stood . . . in dumb and dismal silence," watching millions of acres of Sauk land being ceded to the victorious Americans.

Southward, too, the Indians fell back. In January 1838, a young, valiant Florida Indian leader named Osceola, who had fought to preserve Seminole lands, died in prison in South Carolina. In October of the same year, the Cherokee, who had adopted the white man's ways and even his language, were being herded off their southeastern homelands by the United States

Army on the long Trail of Tears, forced to miserable lands beyond the Mississippi, victims of the Indian Removal Act. Although one tribe after another had been promised a new, permanent homeland with each westward move, safe from white interference, now the Removal Act demanded that they all be resettled west of the Mississippi River.

There was no permanent homeland there, either, once the increasing numbers of pioneers realized that the West was a trove of natural riches—timber, minerals, wildlife. It had been supposed that the land was worthless and therefore the Indians were welcome to it. So, the story west of the Mississippi was a replay of what had gone on before. Indians of the Southwest, the Northwest, the Plains were steadily forced off their lands, hemmed in and rounded up, and given claim to whatever territory the white men did not want. In vain, the Apache, the Navaho, the Sioux, and the Nez Perce struggled to keep some scrap of their forests or prairies. Some, like Chief Joseph of the Nez Perce, who retreated with his people all the way from their beloved Wallowa Valley in Oregon to the Bearpaw Mountains of Montana, tried everything short of war to meet the demands of territorial governors and generals. All went down to ultimate defeat.

The Indian was not the "noble savage" that some romantic writers made him out to be, nor was the white man the totally treacherous villain others claimed. There was bloodletting and barbarism on both sides. The fact remains that today the descendants of the original

American Indians live chiefly on barren reservation land, set aside for them by the United States Government. Though they are not "vanishing Americans" in one sense, since their population is increasing, they are all but vanished as far as their ancient way of life goes. Only in the names of cities, rivers, and mountains are there a reminder of how much the Indian was once a vibrantly living part of the land.

Half of our states have Indian names, and many of our large cities. Wichita . . . Chattanooga . . . Topeka . . . Tacoma . . . Cheyenne . . . Tallahassee . . . Chicago . . . It would take many pages to list even a few of the Indian names that dot our landscape. The struggle of the Indians to keep their homeland was a heroic one. The marvel is that it took the white forces so long—four hundred years—to conquer the comparatively small numbers of native Americans, even with the help of the diseases to which Indians were so vulnerable. Rum and whiskey were also effective in destroying the Indians. But even the most broken-spirited, or those who had aped white ways were torn between new ways and the old, haunted by customs and beliefs of an earlier time.

The boy could hear the sound of the fresh-flowing stream from where he sat and the chatter of a squirrel. They were good sounds, helping to relieve the quietness of the forest glen chosen for the most sacred experience in his twelve years of life. Beside him he had built a pile of stones, as was required by custom, and now he sat by it patiently waiting for the all-important sign. The sign could be a bird, an animal, perhaps only a spinning leaf, but it would come so that at last he could end his vigil of waiting. Without a proper sign from the spirit world that lurked and watched all around him, he would never have his personal guardian spirit or *Wyakin*.

The sun was beginning to set behind the darkening forest trees, the second setting sun since he had come, and he could feel the gathering chill. Cold and darkness did not matter, he told himself. Not even the hunger that gnawed at his stomach—though his thirst was growing intense. He moistened his lips, hearing again the sound of the bright creek, then deliberately ignored it. Because of his hunger and fatigue, he felt dizzy. The last red rays of the sun suddenly seemed blurred, and in their crimson rays he seemed to see the outline of a flaming elk. His heart beat swiftly. It would be a great thing to have a mighty elk as his *Wyakin*. The vision faded, leaving only the red sky.

Clouds whipped across the sunset and the wind rose. The wind had a growling voice, like that of a grizzly. He looked over his shoulder, half fearful, half hopeful. A grizzly *Wyakin* would give him much power. A bird made a rustling noise. If a grouse appeared plainly before him, its spirit welcoming his, he would always be able to hide from danger. A deer would bring speed; a coyote, cunning. He continued to wait. The vision would come—or he would die waiting.

He half dozed when the clouds parted. There, again, the shape of a huge elk appeared, only this time it seemed to be advancing toward him. The boy trembled, his mouth open. There was no doubt this time. The elk was his *Wyakin*, and it was speaking to him, telling him what he needed to know to become strong and wise. He stood up, breathless. It was exactly as the old wise man at the village had told him it would be. Now that he had had his vision, he could return to his home. Always, in the future, the spirit of the elk would protect him. When he went to war, he would be sure to carry a bit of elk hide or a piece of elk antler with him, carefully concealed in a medicine bundle.

The boy happened to be a Nez Perce Indian but his search for a personal guardian spirit was typical of many other Indian tribes. Each man's goal was to seek a vision and so establish contact with some supernatural force, whether buffalo or bear, whirlwind or lightning. And the medicine bundle was his most precious possession. Some of these bundles became the common property of the tribe and were in the keeping of the shamans to be brought out only during the most important ceremonies.

Among the Nez Perce, girls as well as boys could seek their individual *Wyakin*. In most tribes, however, it was the males who went on such quests while women and girls busied themselves with all the necessary chores around the family camp. Women tended the fire, gathered the fuel for it, made the clothing, and prepared the food the hunters brought in. When the family moved camp to follow the bison or deer, to find new fishing grounds, or to attend some tribal gathering, the women also carried most of the baggage. Even little girls went with either babies or firewood strapped to their backs. It was essential for the men to be unburdened, free to strike back in case of attack from an enemy, or able to pursue game if it appeared. Such a division of labor was a practical one. Certain other distinctions between men's and women's work came about as a result of tradition and custom, or as an outgrowth of the different talents of the sexes. It was demeaning for men to do "women's work." But though spinning and weaving might seem to be in this category, it was not so among the Pueblo Indians where men were the spinners and weavers.

It was the Spaniards arriving in the Southwest in 1540 who gave the Pueblo Indians their name because they lived in closely clustered communities somewhat like the *pueblos,* or villages, in Spain. The clay earth, *adobe,* provided materials for house construction, the same substance used by Spanish builders. Such clay and other natural materials also gave what was required for fine pottery.

A major group of the Pueblo Indians in New Mexico is the Zuñi. Before the Zuñi farmer saw or heard of a white man's plow or scientific irrigation methods, he managed to wrest a living from the dry soil. In the spring, the Zuñi planter took his hoe and chopping knife with him to an arroyo he had chosen for his cornfield. An arroyo is a watercourse. In desert regions rain is scarce so that what in spring may be a torrent, through much of the year is a parched gully. Within the sand embankments of the arroyo, the Zuñi carefully cut many forked cedar branches, drove them into the dry stream bed, and then created a dam of boughs, rocks, sticks, and earth. The dam was built across the arroyo and was augmented by secondary dams, each built to hold back whatever water might course down the channel. Once the dams were built, the Indian began a patient search, following the patterns of the ground where former torrents had left their traces. The object he sought was a hardened piece of clay that had been washed from the banks, rolling and rolling in the stream until it became a ball. Finding it, the man took it in his hands, breathed reverently upon it, and then placed it at one side of the stream bed where he most wanted rainfall to overflow. He buried it, gave a proper prayer to the rain gods, and then covered it with a dam similar to the others.

To the Zuñi, the ball of clay was what he called a *ti-kwa*. He and his fellows had a favorite sport in which they kicked a small stick called a *ti-kwa* toward a distant goal, scooping the stick up on their naked toes across a twenty-five-mile course, until the winner racing ahead kicked the stick across the goal mark. A sun-hardened ball of clay in the arroyo, the Zuñi people believed, was the *ti-kwa* plaything of the water gods, which the gods had kicked to the spot with their invisible feet. So, when the first rains came, the water gods would want to find their *ti-kwa* again. By hiding the *ti-kwa* and building his dams in a careful pattern, the Zuñi farmer hoped to tempt the water gods toward his corn hills. When he finished his dams and earth enclosures he joined with others before the corn priest, the keeper of the sacred medicine of his clan. The priest prepared feathered sticks and made the appropriate prayers, beseeching the sky gods to deliver showers that would bring both moisture and new soil to the field.

When rain did come, it was trapped by the cunning system of dikes so that even though the stream might go dry three hours after the downpour, every part of the cornfield was soaked and covered with a fine loam. As a result, the corn sprouted and grew. To the Zuñi planter his prayers and the corn priest's rituals played a vital part, but he was not so impractical as to give up his careful engineering.

Religious ceremony and strict social rituals were basic to Indian life regardless of where they lived or how they procured their food. Newborn infants were almost always welcomed for they added to the strength of the tribe. Among the Omaha Indians the infant was not regarded as a true Omaha until it had been formally welcomed. First of all it was greeted simply as a living creature, a particular expression of the life force that existed throughout nature. When the infant was eight days old, the priest would take his place in the door of the lodging where the infant lay, and raising his right hand to the sky, palm outward, cry to the heavens in a loud, ringing voice. He would ask the sun, moon, and stars to make the path of the newborn child a smooth one. He called to the winds, clouds, rain, and mists, all that moved in the air, to make the path smooth. He called to the hills and valleys, the trees and grasses—and to the birds, animals, and insects—all presences and spirits to make the way smooth so that the child could eventually travel over all obstacles.

Later, when the child was old enough to walk by itself, it was formally introduced to the tribe. Its baby name was discarded, its feet were fitted with new moccasins, and its sacred, Omaha name was announced to all nature and to the assembled people. In moccasins for babies, a hole was always cut so that if a messenger from the spirit world should come and say, "I have come to take you with me," the child could answer, "I cannot go —my moccasins are worn out." The ceremony was the same for boy or girl, but boys had to undergo further rites, in time, to prepare them to be warriors. Among the Omaha this was called "to cut the hair." A lock was cut from the crown of the boy's head, then laid away in a case which was kept as a sacred repository.

Such rituals dealing with the newborn or puberty are common to all peoples, not only primitives. Christian baptism is a ritual concerned with the spiritual well-

being of infants, or even with older persons. Orthodox
Jews make a great occasion of a boy's reaching maturity,
as in the bar mitzvah ceremony. At one time in the United
States, a boy was recognized as adult when he stopped
wearing knee pants and put on long trousers. Today, a
driver's license is a common symbol.

Though there may be some similarities in outward symbols, there is a profound difference between
ancient Indian attitudes and those of most modern cultures. Always, the Indian ceremonies and symbols were
concerned with a spiritual relation to the universe. One of
the chief features in all religious ceremonies was the power
of the word. To be able to give any object, person, or
spirit a name meant to have power over it. Consequently,
many Indians had secret names that they were reluctant
to tell to anyone outside the group, a custom that per-
sists today among certain tribes.

Although early Indians had no written language,
relying on memory, drawings, and pictographs to record
certain events, their oral tradition was rich, myth and
song passed on from generation to generation. Many were
highly skilled orators, and others were natural poets. The
speeches of some chiefs, translated by interpreters and
printed for posterity to read, are often beautifully eloquent.
The same is true of much Indian poetry. Finding one's
own "song," was a vital part of Indian life. It was not
enough to repeat the song of another. One must seek his
own words to express his own visions. Even at death, one
should be prepared with an individual poem of farewell.

But there were songs of joy, too, and lullabies; songs of love and of going to war; songs of grief and worship of nature. Songs were a form of magic, also, which Indians believed could cure the sick, defeat enemies, or make crops grow.

Along with the poems and speeches went legends and storytelling. On winter nights when it was too dark or cold to hunt, or there were no berries or fruits to pick, the father of a family might entertain the children with a legend about the beginning of the world or a famous battle. When grown, his sons and grandsons would repeat the same stories to their children.

The paintings with which Plains Indians decorated their tepees, the symbols drawn in colored sand by the Navahos, the totem poles erected by the Tlingit of the Northwest—these, too, had spiritual and ritual significance, just as the Christian cross, the hammer and sickle, or a national flag has to present-day peoples. Always, the attempt to influence the natural and spirit world was paramount. Some designs such as those in Pueblo pottery or weaving were purely for ornamentation but in most cases there was a symbolic significance.

In the same way that Indians were fearful of revealing their "real" names to strangers or an enemy, they were afraid of having their faces reproduced in a painting or a photograph. The Mohave Indians of southern California were especially fearful of having their pictures made, for in order to go to the great world beyond the sky when they died, they believed it was necessary that their bodies, all their possessions, and any likenesses of them must be destroyed. Otherwise their unhappy spirits would cling to earth. In the early 1900s a photographer made a picture of a dead Indian. He then made a print from the negative and placed it in the showcase of his studio. The Indian's widow saw it, bought it, and burned it. The photographer made another print and displayed that. Again, the desperate widow managed to procure enough money to buy the picture. This went on for several times until white people in the neighborhood went in anger to the photographer, obtained the negative, and destroyed it.

From the beginning of white colonization, Christian missionaries tried to introduce their own religion among the various Indian tribes. Confronted by the white man's power, or seeking food and protection, some Indians abandoned their own beliefs. Others attempted to have the best of two worlds, worshiping the white man's God and their own gods. In one Southwest pueblo, the natives attended the Catholic church and celebrated its festivals, while in secret they practiced their own religious rites in circular earth pits called kivas, or held their masked dances in mountain retreats. For those Indians who clung faithfully to their own religion, Seneca Chief Red Jacket spoke in response to a missionary who had appealed to his people in 1805.

"Friend and brother," he said to the missionary, speaking in Seneca, "it was the will of the Great Spirit that we should meet together this day. He is in all things. . . . He has taken his garment from before the sun, and caused it to shine with brightness upon us. . . . There was a time when our forefathers owned this great island. Their seats extended from the rising to the setting sun. The Great Spirit had made it for the use of the Indians. He had created the buffalo, the deer, and other animals for food. He made the bear and the beaver, and their skins served us for clothing . . . but an evil day came upon us; your forefathers crossed the great waters. . . . Their numbers were small; they found friends, not enemies; they told us they had fled from their own country for fear of wicked men, and came here to enjoy their religion. . . . We gave them corn and meat; they gave us poison in return. . . . Wars took place; Indians were hired to fight against Indians, and many of our people were destroyed. They also brought strong liquors among us; it was strong and powerful and has slain thousands.

"Brother . . . you have now become a great people and we have scarcely left a place to spread our blankets; you have got our country but you are not satisfied; you want to force your religion upon us. . . .

"We also have a religion which was given to our forefathers. . . . It teaches us to be thankful for all the favors we receive; to love each other, and to be united.

"Brother, the Great Spirit has made us all; but he has made a great difference between his white and red children; he has given us a different complexion, and different customs. . . . Since he has made so great a difference between us in other things, why may we not conclude that he has given us different religion according to our understanding? . . . Brother, we do not wish to destroy your religion, or take it from you; we only want to enjoy our own."

After Red Jacket was finished, he and other Indians went to the missionary to take his hand in friendship. The missionary rose hastily, saying that there could be no fellowship between the religion of God and the works of the devil, and left.

Not all missionaries were so small-minded. Many were kind, patient, and courageous, truly believing that they were bringing salvation to misguided savages. It was not an easy task, even for the best, to convert Indians to the white man's faith when the same whites were plundering the Indians' lands and driving the red man into want, starvation, and disease.

After the Indian Removal Act of 1830, almost all Indians were cleared from the East. Some such as the Chickasaw, Choctaw, and Cherokee went voluntarily, having no choice. Sent westward by government agents, they were ". . . half-convinced and half-compelled," going to "inhabit new deserts where the importunate whites will not let them remain ten years in peace. In this manner do the Americans obtain, at a very low price, whole provinces which the richest sovereigns of Europe could not purchase."

Such was the conclusion of the French politician and writer Alexis de Tocqueville, who visited the young United States in the 1830s and wrote his impressions. He happened to be in Memphis on the day when a ragged group of Choctaw, part of thousands who had agreed to be transported from their homelands, embarked across the Mississippi River toward the promise of a new life. A new death it proved to be, in most cases.

"The Indians had their families with them, and they brought in their train the wounded and the sick, with children newly born and old men upon the verge of death. . . . I saw them embark to pass the mighty river, and never will that solemn spectacle fade my remembrance. No cry, no sob, was heard among the assembled crowd; all was silent. Their calamities were of an ancient date, and they knew them to be irremediable."

Once the Eastern Indians were banished to the plains and prairies of the West, the same story of land rape by the whites was repeated. Added to the Indians' sufferings were epidemics brought on by lack of resistance to white men's diseases. Out of 1600 Mandan Indians, only a hundred survived a smallpox epidemic, and they are today extinct. Yet, George Catlin who stayed with them on the upper Missouri described them as a happy, peaceful people, their village "one of the most beautiful and pleasing that can be seen in the world. . . ."

With the whites' appropriation of woodland and stream, the animals on which Indians depended for food and clothing also disappeared. One of the most tragic instances of this was the destruction of the bison of the Great Plains. For countless generations these shaggy beasts had supplied the plains-dwelling Indians with food, shelter, clothing, and even fuel in the form of bison droppings, called buffalo chips. The bison numbered in the millions and they were the life blood of the Plains tribes, especially of the Sioux who became the largest and strongest and wildest of all the Plains Indians. By treaty with the United States Government, the Sioux gave up a great part of their former territory, which extended from Minnesota to the Rocky Mountains, and from the Yellowstone to the Platte, being promised that what is now the state of South Dakota would be "set apart for their absolute and undisturbed use and occupation." The government agreed that they would be allowed to hunt within their old range, outside the limits of the reservation, so long as the bison herds remained.

The bison, the Indians believed, would last forever. Always their mighty herds had crowded the land, pawing and snorting, raising new calves, making the earth tremble with their hoofs. In the meantime, government agents moved among the Indians, promising rations, cattle, doctors, farmers, and teachers to educate them to the white man's way of life. All this sounded good to the Sioux, so when the whites asked permission to route a railroad through their "absolute and undisturbed" domain, they agreed.

The rails and the puffing "iron horse" invaded the land of the bison. Hunters and emigrants swarmed onto the plains. Men like Buffalo Bill slaughtered bison recklessly to provide meat for the railroad crews, or to furnish sport for rich game hunters. Scarcely before the Sioux realized what was happening, the bison herds dwindled. Whereas the Indians had used every scrap of buffalo meat, hide, and horn for useful purposes, white hunters took only prize portions such as the tongue or the hide and left the carcass to rot.

In the wake of the disappearing bison came another catastrophe, from the Indian point of view. Gold was discovered on the reservation, in the Black Hills, and miners and lawless desperadoes rushed into the country, defying the protesting Indians and the government.

Their bison gone, their land invaded, the desperate Sioux and their Cheyenne allies struck back. In one of their last successful stands, they defeated the forces under Lieutenant Colonel George Custer at the Little Bighorn River in Montana, in June, 1876. Delirious with victory over the man they called the "squaw killer," they massacred Custer's two hundred and twenty-five troops. After long frustration and despair, the Indians and their leaders Sitting Bull and Crazy Horse believed the tide had turned. Actually, the victory was the beginning of the end for the embattled red men. At the stunning news of Custer's defeat, whites were determined to have their revenge and rid the continent of Indians for once and for all.

The whites had already succeeded in crushing the southern Plains tribes in 1874. The Nez Perce were next, in 1877, the Utes in 1879, and the Apaches through much of the 1880s until Geronimo surrendered with his little band of thirty-six survivors. Then, in 1890, came the last serious Indian resistance. Again the Sioux, under Sitting Bull, attempted to regain their lost birthright. The result was the massacre of more than three hundred Sioux, chiefly women and children, at Wounded Knee, South Dakota. It was the end of military resistance for the American Indian.

After the defeat of the Nez Perce, their fine leader, Chief Joseph, gave voice to the general sorrow of all Indians. To the victorious white officers, he said in his surrender speech, "I am tired of fighting. Our chiefs are killed. . . . The old men are all dead. It is the young men who say yes or no. He who led the young men is dead. It is cold and we have no blankets. The little children are freezing to death. My people, some of them, have run away to the hills, and have no blankets, no food; no one knows where they are—perhaps freezing to death. I want to have time to look for my children and see how many I can find. Maybe I shall find them among the dead. Hear me, my chiefs, I am tired; my heart is sick and sad. From where the sun now stands, I will fight no more forever."

Chief Joseph kept his word and died, a broken-hearted exile far from the Wallowa Valley that he had loved and fought for.

Only in the central part of the present state of Alaska were the Indians left relatively untouched by the white advance. There, and in the interior of western Canada, the Athabaskan Indians followed the migrations of the caribou, as some still do, using the animal's flesh for food, its skin for clothing. Whereas the Eskimo population usually wintered on the seashore, the Indians found their shelter in the forest. In summer, the two groups sometimes met as their hunters ventured into each other's territory, and generally they were hostile to each other. The most distinctive article of the Athabaskans is the *babiche,* a caribou or deerskin thong cut to an amazing length from the whole skin of the animal, and used for everything from lacing snowshoes to making nets. These Indians of the northern forests developed the making of snowshoes and toboggans into an art, and white men modeled their own equipment on these.

Another Indian group, coast dwellers and sea-farers, were master wood carvers. These were the Tlingit Indians of the Pacific Northwest, especially of southeastern Alaska. Builders, basket makers, warriors, they depended mainly on the sea for food, and their villages were rows of large houses on posts, facing the water. The shores of the mainland and the numerous coastal islands where they lived were forested with large cedar trees, and it was these trees that the Tlingit carved into ornate totem poles. Such poles were adorned with stylized faces and figures, one above the other, to indicate the ancestral lineage and myths associated with a particular clan. Just as an American child is born into a certain family group including grandmothers, aunts, cousins, so each Tlingit was. But the Tlingit child was also born into a clan—the beaver clan, raven, wolf, owl, or whatever particular creature was recognized in the legends of the clan's ancestors. Neighboring Indian tribes also made such totem poles but the Tlingit are the best known for this art. They were skilled craftsmen in lumbering and they used slabs cut from cedar trees for spacious houses. Cedar was also used for dugouts both small and large, and the shredded inner bark for weaving into maps and capes. Their carving extended beyond totem poles to huge wooden masks, canoe bows, house posts, and smaller articles such as spoons and rattles. Their ceremonial costumes were brilliant in color and design, and elaborate rituals were the order of the day.

Like other totem pole makers of the Pacific coastal regions, the Tlingit practiced the "potlatch," the giving of a feast on special occasions such as marriage or the birth of a child, and distributing property to all the guests assembled. The potlatch was primarily a redistributive economic system. The more the host gave away—and his gifts could include slaves, as the Tlingit kept war captives, or Indians purchased from other tribes, as servants —the more highly regarded the host was. There were strict social relations, the chiefs at the top, the slaves at the bottom. Also high in order were the shamans, or medicine men, who were believed to have direct contact with the supernatural powers.

Unlike the natives of the northernmost coasts and frozen tundra, the Tlingit could go about scantily dressed or naked in the moist, mild climate, though robes of sea otter or woven bark were common. The main food was fish, especially salmon, supplemented by berries, roots, and bulbs. Fish and meat were dried and smoked and accumulated in large stores for the lavish feasts.

Until the 1880s the Tlingit's main contact with outside civilization came through fur traders and whalers. As the Tlingit found most of their food at sea, they could not easily be "fenced in" by the whites. However, fish canneries were established by the whites, missions were built, and gradually the Tlingit began to turn to a cash economy, taking jobs in the canneries or supplying the fish for them in exchange for money. Traditions weakened and the art of totem pole carving died out. In one island village, Kake, Alaska, in the early 1900s, the natives burned every totem pole there. This was done because Christian missionaries convinced the people that a totem culture was not desirable.

In 1967, the year of the Alaska Purchase Centennial, the Kake villagers decided to revitalize their totem-building tradition. Lack of money and the difficulty of finding capable carvers delayed the project. But, in the summer of 1969, the work was going ahead so that a cedar totem pole 130 feet tall was a part of Alaska's exhibit at the 1970 Expo in Japan.

After the First World War, government administrators applied strict laws against the potlatch custom, believing that such ceremonies in which goods were sometimes deliberately squandered or even destroyed were a waste of the Indians' natural resources. Today, the Tlingit live on the marginal fringes of the white man's economy, wearing white men's clothes, copying white men's ways, and though a form of the potlatch tradition lingers it has little resemblance to the past.

For the Tlingit, as for most Indians, the past is a vague memory, even though some contemporary young leaders are trying to revive ancient glories and even return to certain ways of Indian life. For the most part, except in museums, the totem poles and the grave posts containing the ashes of ancestors are gone. Gone, too, are the wigwams and feathered headdresses of the Plains Indians, the long houses of the Iroquois, the arrow and tomahawk, the excitements of the hunts or raids, the birchbark canoe, the campfires and living legends. Gone, or rapidly vanishing, are wild creatures the Great Spirit provided for his children. And gone are the days when an Indian boy would choose to go and sit in solitude, fasting in wait for a vision. Or if he does go on such a quest, what hope is there for his future or that of any Indian?

At one time, the chief hope of most white people was that the American Indian would somehow disappear, whether by dying out or by being completely absorbed into white society. In pioneer days, the first attitude was the dominant one, expressed in the saying "The only good Indian is a dead Indian." There were charitable groups and individuals who did not feel this way, but did all they could to try to alleviate the Indians' desperate situation. The government passed what it considered to be fair and reasonable laws for protection of the beleagured tribes, but even the best laws fell before the greed and self-interest of land-hungry frontiersmen, and their political representatives. Reservations of land set aside for the dispossessed Indians were often little better than desolate concentration camps from which no Indian could wander without a special permit. Some were enclosed with barbed wire. Indian agents placed in charge, white overseers, varied from kind to indifferent to cruel. Under the latter there was systematic persecution and even murder.

For all that many whites wished that the Indian would disappear, he did not. Stubbornly he clung to life, in spite of hunger, disease, and humiliation. As a result, a policy of assimilation became dominant. From one federal administration to the next, funds were appropriated to support policies that would, hopefully, change Indians from being wards of the state to independent wage earners. In order to change the Indian into a white man in all except his skin color, authorities suppressed tribal customs and native councils, and sent the children, sometimes by force, to all-Indian schools in distant cities. Some of these children managed, in time, to become assimilated into the white culture, but the great majority returned to the reservations, homesick, bewildered, dispirited, while others wandered through city slums, lost to any productive way of life.

Not until 1924 were Indians granted citizenship; this came by way of recognition of the services volunteered by Indians in World War I. During World War II, about twenty-five thousand Indians served in the armed forces of the United States. Those with a knowledge of their native tongue were especially valuable as communications teams, being able to talk on field telephones or walkie-talkie radios in a language utterly unknown to the enemy.

Some of these servicemen, away from the reservation for the first time, returned home with ambitions to bring the white man's technology to their own people, but such plans were usually crushed because of the lack of money and opportunity, or because they were not wanted. Other Indians, in the scarce labor market, found work in war plants and shipyards and a number adapted themselves to white ways, though still retaining their identity as Indians. By 1969, thousands of Indians were concentrating in cities, a majority being in the Los Angeles and southern California's Orange County. Overall, the largest centers of Indian population are first Arizona, then Oklahoma, followed by New Mexico, Alaska, California, North Carolina, South Dakota, Montana, and Washington.

The American Indian population as a whole is estimated to be around six hundred thousand, more than twice the figure at the time of World War I. So, the Indian is not vanishing but is, in fact, our fastest growing minority.

Beneath these seemingly reassuring statistics, there are others that show that the Indian is the most distressed minority population in the United States. It is not the number of lives that is the ultimate value but the quality of each individual life. And for the majority of Indians, that quality is desperately low.

The Indian has the highest suicide rate among young persons, especially teen-age girls and boys. Most often this is because of a feeling of frustration and hopelessness. The school dropout rate is high, as much as

50 per cent in some areas. A recent survey of 1200 Indian students of the Southwest showed a dropout rate of 38.7 per cent, 6 per cent above the national average. To put it another way, the Indian completes about five years of schooling whereas all other Americans average about eleven years. One of the factors that discourages Indian students is that too many teachers believe that the best these youngsters can do is to become wage laborers. The Indians themselves begin to see themselves in the same way. Most manage well academically, staying on a par with non-Indian classmates, up to the fifth or sixth grade. Then they begin to fall behind, largely because they are impressed with the conviction that they are second-class citizens and lose whatever motivation they may have had to strive for excellence.

As one Nevada high school girl, lonely and bitter in a boarding school far from her home, expressed it, "If you don't do well in school it doesn't matter because they never expect you to, anyhow." She described the school she went to as like a prison, everything done by the bell, the matrons watching every move in the halls or outside through binoculars. There was no mixing of the sexes at lunch, the boys seated on one side, the girls on the other. If a boy and girl were discovered holding hands or exchanging notes, punishment came in the form of scrubbing floors or cleaning latrines.

Lacking in most schools is any concern with Indian history or the Indian language. In the Blackfoot school district in Idaho, three fourths of the students in elementary school are Indian, yet every teacher is white. Speaking the Indian language is prohibited. The late Senator Robert Kennedy visited the district in 1968 and asked whether Indian culture and traditions were taught. He was told, "There is no history to this tribe." When he asked if there were any books on Indian culture in the library, he was shown one with a cover illustrating the scalping of a white child by an Indian.

More than half the Indian people live on approximately two hundred reservations in tin-roofed shacks, leaky adobe huts, tar-papered hovels, and even junked automobiles. Unemployment ranges between 40 and 75 per cent, the average annual income being around $1500. The average life span is short, forty-two years; for whites it is sixty-eight. In California, a 1966 survey showed that water from contaminated sources was used in around 40 per cent of the homes and had to be hauled under unsanitary conditions by 40 to 50 per cent of all Indian families. The incidence of tuberculosis is seven times that of the American population as a whole. There has, however, been progress in health and sanitation since the United States Public Health Service took over responsibility for these in 1955, especially among the Navahos.

The chief agency responsible for Indian welfare is the Bureau of Indian Affairs, originally under the direction of the War Department, but functioning today under the Department of the Interior. When it was founded a century ago, the BIA was instructed to remove Indian children "from their native culture and language so they could take their place in modern society. . . ." Federal funds meant for Indians were handled by BIA agents and frequently it was the agents who benefited, not the red man. Says the successful song writer, musician, and singer Buffy Sainte Marie, a Cree Indian raised by white foster parents, "The Bureau represents the Government, not the Indians." Other Indian spokesmen think that without the BIA the Indians would be worse off. Bitterness, dependence, and hope alternate in the Indian attitudes toward the Bureau. Certainly, in the earlier days of the BIA there was considerable corruption and cruelty. When John Collier became the commissioner, serving from 1933 to 1945, he made sweeping reforms in line with his dedication to the Indian cause. Even so, the BIA, for all it strives to elect the proper course, remains a large bureaucracy in which even the most dedicated persons can lose their way. Good will bogs down in the machinery, and not even the fact that two native Indians have held the commissionership successively has brought any dramatic change for the better.

One source of bitterness among many Indians was the government's termination policy under which certain reservations were officially abandoned. The BIA attempted to deal with these "terminated" Indians by providing young Indians with a one-way trip to urban centers for job training and education. Too often these Indians could not adapt to alien and confusing surroundings, far from relatives and friends, and ended up more discouraged than ever. The termination program has been temporarily halted, but Indians are skeptical of what will follow.

In recent years the cry of "Red Power" has joined that of "Black Power," and militant groups of Indians have joined together to demand more opportunity and a better chance at equality. Among them are separatists who want a separate Indian nation within the United States. One breakthrough occurred following a Capital Conference on Indian Poverty in Washington, 1964, which brought the assistance of the Office of Economic Opportunity to the reservations. For the first time, once programs initiated by Indians themselves had been approved, funds were made available to the Indians to use according to their own best judgment. Encouraged, feeling new pride, the Indians proved that they could handle their own affairs better than most outsiders simply because they understood their own problems better. Whatever gradual improvement has taken place is due in part to the Indians' attempts to bring pressure to bear on governmental agencies and on Congress. Their National Congress of American Indians was founded in 1944, the spearhead of a political movement to achieve a better life for Indians. Other organizations, including the National Indian Youth Council and such governmental organizations as the Interior Department's Indian Arts and Crafts Board, are working to restore the Indian's pride in his arts and traditions. Under the latter agency, the Institute of American Indian Arts was created in 1960. Located in Santa Fe, New Mexico, the Institute offers training in nearly every field of the arts—painting, ceramics, textiles, music, creative writing—to native American youth from all areas of the United States. Applicants must be at least one-fourth degree of Indian, Eskimo, or Aleut ancestry. Tuition, board, and art materials are furnished free to accepted students.

In late November 1969, a group of some seventy young Indians made an attempt to bring the nation's attention to the plight of the Indians when they slipped past Coast Guard boats and landed on the island of Alcatraz in San Francisco Bay. The island, the site of a crumbling federal prison closed down in 1963, had been abandoned and no definite use for it had been agreed upon. The Indian "invaders" demanded that the island be turned over to them under the provisions of the 1868 Sioux Treaty, stating that the treaty provides that an unused federal land reverts automatically to the Indians. The peaceful occupation of Alcatraz was at first regarded as a joke by outsiders, but as more Indians arrived, representing thirty tribes, it was generally realized that the Indians were serious. They wished to create a cultural-educational center financed, but not controlled, by the federal government. More than a year later, a determined group of Indians remained on the island, huddled together in the empty cell blocks, building fires against the fog-laden winter chill, depending on support from the mainland for all their supplies, including drinking water, still demanding that the government accede to their demands.

The feeling of the group was expressed by a spokesman who said, "The Indians have the arrow, and with Alcatraz they have put a point on the arrow. We've been pushed around—now we are trying to do something for ourselves."

The newer Indian militants are seeking their own identity as native Americans and they have the same disdain for those of their race who imitate white ways that the militant blacks have. These blacks call such persons "Uncle Toms"; the Indians refer to such individuals in their ranks as "Uncle Tomahawks." Splinter groups have broken off from the National Indian Youth Council, professing views so radical that their critics call them "Red Muslims." However, for the first time since the early, farseeing chiefs tried to band the tribes together, present-day tribes are struggling to paper over their differences in a common cause. There are some 263 separate Indian tribes, bands, villages, pueblos, and groups in states other than Alaska, plus 300 native Alaskan communities.

The battle against being assimilated or culturally annihilated by white culture is not new; ancestral chiefs attempted to resist that fate. Others tried valiantly to adapt to white ways, like the Cherokee, but were disinherited just the same. Among the most successful in preserving old ways are the Hopis and other pueblo peoples of the Southwest who manage to maintain their priesthoods, dances, and social and political organizations with little change. Non-Christian Mohawks of New York, some of whom live and work in urban centers, particularly in construction, cling to a revised form of their ancient faith. They frequently return to their reservations and may have a family there.

Some tribes have realized financial profits from their reservation holdings. The Menominees of Wisconsin, for instance, developed a profitably operating commercial forest; then because they were financially well off, they were among the tribes terminated by the government. The result of the hasty and ill-conceived termination was disastrous to the Menominees as millions of dollars of tribal assets disappeared almost overnight in the rush to transform the reservation to a completely self-supporting county. In contrast, the discovery of oil on the land of some of the Osages in Oklahoma brought a great deal of money to these Indians in land leases. This was more a disaster than a benefit as the formerly impoverished Indians lacked the ability to use their sudden riches profitably, and most squandered the money buying white men's wares in the form of expensive cars or other symbols of status. Land rights in the California desert area of Palm Springs brought wealth to some of the Cahuilla Indians. Oil, gas, and minerals discovered on the lands of the Navahos have provided the tribal council with capital, which has been invested by those Indians to benefit the tribe.

The Navahos are more numerous than any of the other Indian groups north of Mexico, numbering around 117,000. They live in the semiarid regions of Arizona, New Mexico, and Utah. In spite of money from oil and mineral leases, the Navaho economy is critical. Its increasing population cannot subsist on the barren land used for grazing. The sheep herds on which they largely depend for survival must be cut back because the land cannot support them. The old crafts such as weaving beautiful blankets and rugs are slowly being abandoned. In spite of their comparative success so far in maintaining their traditional social structure, there is a steadily lessening regard for old disciplines. As the present-day Navaho medicine men, the singers of chants, and practitioners of sacred and painting rites die off, few are trained to take their place.

In spite of efforts within enlightened Indian communities and among white supporters to preserve the best of the native American heritage, past ways are slowly eroding. The roots have been torn from their natural earth and can only be kept alive by deliberate and even artificial means. Though not vanishing, and perhaps even finding a breakthrough into equal citizenship, the American Indian of the future is bound to be a far different person from the days when Spaniards first rode through the Kansas buffalo grass, or the Pilgrims landed on the cold shores at Plymouth.

2.
Land of the Northern Lights

ESKIMOS AND ALEUTS

There were no fires and no shelters on the ice shelf where the Eskimo skin boat stood, its prow projecting over the water at the edge of the ice. All the whaling gear was ready, the floats, upright paddles, and harpoon. Nearby, the fur-clad Eskimo hunters waited for the first sight of a whale. It was late March. The snowbirds, harbingers of the whales, had already appeared over the Alaskan coast north of the Bering Strait, and now the crew members took turns scanning the cold blue water beyond the ice.

The ceremonial whale dances had been held in the village before the men set out, and all the proper songs sung to bring good luck. The gear had been scraped clean in order to please the whale so that he would permit himself to be taken. An ivory harpoon with a cutting edge of slate glistened in the pale sunlight, a long thong of walrus hide attached to its shaft. The head of the harpoon was ingeniously devised to remain embedded in the whale's body while detaching itself from the shaft so that the shaft attached to a skin float could be recovered.

One hunter apart from the rest chanted a prayerful song under his breath, one he had created himself. If the others heard the words, the song would lose its power. With a good song and the charms in the boat— the piece of obsidian chipped into the shape of a small whale, and the skin of a raven—surely this whale season would be a good one. All the people of the village would feast on the catch, young and old, wise and foolish alike. And the hunter could walk with pride.

Whale, caribou, seal, walrus, fish, birds, and birds' eggs—the arctic world was full of riches. Still, there were bad times when the whales did not arrive as expected, or the ice conditions were wrong, or the inland caribou strangely left their usual migration trails. Those were the times of famine. Occasionally, they were so bad that certain villagers had been forced to kill their dogs in order to eat, even though dogs were the natives' most precious possession. Without dog teams it was difficult to haul sleds over the ice and snow. And without sleds the boats could not easily be transported to the hunting grounds, or the slabs of meat brought back to the village.

The chanting hunter searched the open water, looking for the misty spout of a whale as it surfaced to breathe. Then, on a distant ice shelf, he saw human figures; beyond was the hulk of a sailing ship. Smoke puffed out of the tin pipe of a cookstove. The hunter turned and ran toward his companions. White men in search of whales were here again, he reported. The others turned, staring at the distant camp.

More and more white whalers were coming to the Arctic Ocean, their big ships plowing through the ice floes. In 1848, an American vessel from New York had appeared, following some earlier ships, and since then the American whalers had increased steadily.

In the beginning, the Eskimos had considered the white men extremely stupid. They did not even know how to speak the Eskimo language! And their memory was so poor they had to write things down on slips of paper in order to keep track of events. Nor did they do any special dances in honor of the whale, or return the whale's skull to the sea as custom demanded.

The Eskimo hunters talked about the stupidities and shortcomings of the whites, but at the same time they agreed that the steel knives the whites possessed were extremely useful. One of the men in the Eskimo crew had traded some fox skins for one, and the other men had to admit that it was more efficient than their own flint blade knives with bone handles. Against that were some of the cheap goods the whites had brought—cloth that wore out far faster than a caribou or walrus hide. The Eskimos were superior; no doubt about it. Yet, the hunter who had first spied the white whalers' camp felt a certain uneasiness.

A companion shouted that a whale had surfaced in the icy water. At once, the hunters rushed to the skin boat, *umiak*, launched it, and set out in pursuit. The harpooner took his place while the others rowed to over-take the bowhead whale, trying to guess where the crea-ture would emerge again so that the harpoon could sink into its dark flesh. After some twenty minutes, the whale's blunt snout broke the water. At the same time, a boat from the white whaling camp approached swiftly. The Eskimo with the harpoon raised his arm, muscles tense, taking his aim. Just as he was ready to plunge the weapon at its huge target, there was an explosive burst from the other boat. There, a man with a shoulder gun, had shot a bomb at the whale. The creature thrashed toward the bottom, the bomb implanted in its body. There was a muffled boom; in a moment the water was crimson from the whale's blood.

The Eskimo crew watched in dismay as the white men drew on the line fastened to the detached harpoon, pulling the booty toward their whale boat. Then they looked sidewise at each other. The stupid white man, ugly and ignorant, apparently using no special charms to lure the whale, had succeeded in snatching the prize al-most out of their hands. Though the white man's landing boats were clumsy compared to the resilient *umiaks,* their firing sticks were undeniably powerful.

Doubts began to trouble many of the Eskimo natives, especially as the whaling ships, sailing vessels first, then steam powered, increased their activity. Growing numbers of natives began to acquire white men's goods, including such things as tea, flour, tobacco, and rum. Even though they clung to their old rituals, they saw that the white man's whale bombs and darting guns consistently proved more successful than their own Stone Age weapons. And though the foreigners violated all the traditions of the Eskimo, he went unpunished by the spirit gods. He was, in fact, rewarded by shiploads of whales, so much so that the vast herds were disappearing. Other valuable creatures such as fur seals, too, were growing scarce in the face of the white man's awesome weapons.

The Russians had been the first to reach Alaska, coming by way of the Aleutian Islands. There, in 1741, they had discovered massive colonies of sea otters whose rich, soft fur was so valuable the otters were called "swimming gold." Soon, ships from Siberia began making regular journeys to the long chain of rocky islands, the crews killing the otters, blue foxes, and fur seals by the thousands. Though the Russians had superior weapons, they found that natives living on the islands were far more expert at killing otters, and even whales, than they were.

Unlike the Eskimos on the mainland, the Aleuts needed no dog sleds for they were primarily sea hunters. Using *bidarki,* skin-covered boats with circular openings that fitted closely around their bodies, they could move with swiftness toward their prey. Then they would encircle their victims with their canoes and drive home their spears, or use throwing sticks with which they propelled barbed, bone darts. To protect themselves from the spray and the wet fogs of the islands, they used the intestines of whales and bird skins for waterproof parkas. They had no flint, but used stone for their tools. Nor did they have clay for pottery; and, lacking trees, they had only driftwood for building purposes. There was lush vegetation of other kinds, however, from which they made exquisite grass baskets, capes, mats, and shrouds to wrap around their dead. Designs were woven in, the fibers dyed in octopus "ink," and vegetable stains, or with small feathers and colored gut strings.

The Aleuts appear to be among the first Eskimos to arrive in North America, and they spread along the thousand-mile length of the Aleutian Island chain. They had permanent villages. The main part of each house was below ground surface, sod packed around the whale-bone and driftwood frame. Each house was large enough to shelter several families. Animal gut was used for windows. The Aleuts believed that light was a life-giving source and that no one should sleep during daytime. Moving water was believed to be a source of strength, so newborn babies were dipped into the surf, no matter what the time of year, to assure physical stamina.

At the time the Russians began their hunting expeditions, the Aleuts outnumbered all other natives of what is now Alaska, with a population estimated at twenty-five thousand. Because the Russians had trouble maneuvering their heavy landing boats close to pods of the much desired otters, they forced the Aleuts to hunt for them, using bribery, threats, brutality, and even mass murder. They killed so many Aleuts that in less than one hundred years there were fewer than twenty-five hundred left. Other white men came, bringing with them disease germs against which the natives had little resistance. A smallpox epidemic in 1848 raged through the villages, reducing the number of Aleuts to around nine hundred. During World War II, the Japanese invaded the islands and killed most of the population that was left, or transported them as labor forces to Japan.

Today, the Aleuts are a fast vanishing people. Only a few full-blood Aleuts survive, and the old ways are almost entirely forgotten.

The Aleuts' Eskimo relatives in Alaska and those inhabiting the arctic and subarctic regions of Canada, Greenland, and Labrador share many similarities in their culture in spite of their widespread locations. A common factor is the harsh climate. For six to nine months of the year, Eskimos have to cope with severe cold, ice, and snow. Only by extreme ingenuity, patience, and courage have they been able to survive. Using ingenious, highly specialized weapons, the Eskimo became a supreme hunter, combining wits and brawn to take the whales, seals, bears, so necessary for food, clothing, and fuel.

Many people think that all Eskimos live in dome-shaped snowhouses called igloos. The word "igloo" simply means house; only the nomadic Eskimos of central Canada make any kind of permanent house from snow blocks. The coastal-dwelling Eskimos, the majority, live in combination sod and driftwood—or whalebone—framed houses, or sometimes shelters made of stones placed over excavated earth. In the summer, when these Eskimos rove inland in search of fresh-water fish or other game, tents of animal skins are adequate.

"Eskimo" means eater of raw meat. Indian neighbors of the Eskimo disapproved of such a diet but it was the eating of raw whale meat or seal, even including the entrails, that provided the Eskimo with needed vitamins in a world where green plants or berries were scarce. The Athabaskan Indians, dwellers of the Alaska interior, and the coastal-dwelling Eskimos were hostile to each other. There was hostility between certain Eskimo tribes, also, but for the most part the key word for survival among the grinding ice floes, blizzards, and sub-zero temperatures was cooperation. When an Eskimo hunter caught a whale, the flesh was carefully divided according to an age-old pattern, the captain of the crew receiving the choice portion, the rest being divided among others. Whatever the circumstances, the whole village shared in the catch, whether it was whale, ptarmigan, or seal. Such sharing was necessary for the survival of people under harsh conditions.

Consequently, the concept of private property was quite different from that in modern, industrialized countries, though certain articles were regarded as exclusively the property of the user. A soapstone pot, for instance, was regarded as belonging to the wife, as was her slate knife, or *ulu*. But what wealth of food or hides there was, was shared, and it was a proud hunter who could bring home food sufficient for all. There was a realistic give-and-take that included wife sharing with each other, or even with white travelers. However, the wife was always asked her permission. Outsiders interpreted such practices as evidence of low moral standards. Actually, they were highly structured and existed for practical reasons, as to protect the woman and family when the husband had to be away from home on a prolonged trip.

Stealing was practically unknown. If someone in need helped himself to another Eskimo's boat or dog team, it was considered borrowing, and the borrower was expected to return the goods when he was able to.

Pride and loyalty to the family or village were strong among the aboriginal Eskimo. The family could include an almost infinite number of persons through in-laws, cousins, second and third cousins, down to the slimmest of blood or marriage relationships. Definite rules and customs governed marriage although there was no formal, public ceremony. In earlier days, tattoo marks on a woman's face, particularly on the chin, indicated her married status.

Eskimo children were remarkably well behaved, and whippings or even slappings were all but unknown. Deaths from accidents, famine, and old age were frequent, and infants were usually welcomed. However, there were times when starvation confronted families and infants, particularly females, were left outside to perish. Similarly, old persons who had outlived their usefulness would separate from the group to die alone. Infanticide happened only under the extremest circumstances. Otherwise, children were fondled and cherished and treated with respect. Girls learned to be little mothers to the younger offspring, and helpmates to the women of the group, for the women had much to do. It was they who had to sew the skins needed for clothing, the skin boats and tents, and their ingenuity was as great as that of the male hunters. Using animal sinews or even fibers pulled from shank bones of the caribou, they stitched miraculously waterproof seams. When making *mukluks,* the soft, waterproof boots of the Eskimo, they chewed the skins of hair seal or caribou into the necessary softness with their teeth. And each night they chewed boots or other apparel, already worn, to keep them pliable. It was their job, too, to keep the seal blubber lamps and stoves burning for light and warmth. And during the time of the coming of the fish called tomcod, they sat patiently over holes in the ice, deftly hooking and then winding in their catch.

White travelers who had to seek shelter among the Eskimos were astonished at the warmth of the winter shelters. These were normally small because of the need to conserve heat. An entire family, seldom very large as a group living together, but including grandmothers, grandfathers, or uncles, and the rest, would crowd into the small space, sleeping side by side, or sitting in a circle

(1) Feathers and elegant beadwork make for a handsome Sioux.

(2) Once the drummer begins, these Blackfoot Indians will start their dance.

(3) The Navaho weaver's loom looks crude, but from it will come a beautiful rug.

MUSEUM OF THE AMERICAN INDIAN, HEYE FOUNDATION

(4) No room for big brother in this Chippewa baby's cradle board.

BUREAU OF INDIAN AFFAIRS, U.S. DEPARTMENT OF THE INTERIOR

(5) A transistor radio keeps a young Navaho sheepherder company.

(6)
The masks and even the tattoos are works of art among the North Pacific Coast Haida.

(7) Three Pima-Maricopa children of Arizona's Salt River Reservation are getting a "Head Start" in writing.

(8) The winter ice is breaking up, time for the Alaskan Eskimo to hunt for whales.

WIEN CONSOLIDATED AIRLINES
PHOTO BY FRANK WHALEY

(9) The piece of ivory this Eskimo is carving with his bow-and-mouth drill will become an elegant figurine. The Eskimos of Little Diomede Island are experts in such carving.

ALASKA TRAVEL DIVISION

(10) The walrus is very important to the Eskimos of Alaska; here they do a dance to the animal.

(11) A combination of old and new shows in the costumes of these Alaskan Indians: the nose arrow and white man's trousers, the ceremonial capes and ordinary leather shoes.

(12) The Aleut hunters are rainproof inside their hooded coats made from the intestines of whales.

(13) In Siberia, warm furs are welcome to both young and old Chukchi Eskimos.

COURTESY OF THE AMERICAN
MUSEUM OF NATURAL HISTORY

(14) A Pacific Northwest totem pole still stands, its handsome designs contrasting with the barren setting of weeds, wires, and telephone poles.

BUREAU OF INDIAN AFFAIRS,
U.S. DEPARTMENT
OF THE INTERIOR

around a common kettle while they shared meals. Privacy was unknown. No partitions separated parents from children, brothers from sisters. Consequently, youngsters needed no special education to give them an understanding of the sex life of adult human beings.

The husband was the head of the family, but in most cases marriage was a working partnership, the skills of each partner badly needed. Rarely, an Eskimo male might be well off enough to provide for two or more wives. At the same time, he usually took on the support of most of the people in his village who required help, and so became the head man of the community. Usually, such a person was also a medicine man and so had much influence.

Whatever the Eskimos had, they created from the materials at hand. Long before milk was brought north in cans, the women used intestines of seal as containers for reindeer or mother's milk. Or they would make a broth of fish or meat, fill a short length of cleaned intestine with it, and hang it around their necks to keep it warm for the infant's next feeding. Fish nets, berry buckets, fishing sticks, needles, carving knives, all were made by hand. The small boat, the *kayak,* one of the most versatile vessels ever invented, was used by the men, as were the dog sleds with whale bone runners. Men also specialized in ivory carving, using the tusks of walruses for this, but walruses were not found everywhere.

One place where the animals were abundant was the island of Little Diomede in the Bering Strait. This island, the farthest west tip of the North American continent, is only three miles from Big Diomede, which belongs to Russia. There and in neighboring Siberia live the Eskimos of the Soviet Far East, the Chukchi. In the early days of the whaling fleets there were friendly relations between these primitive people and the American Eskimos. Even as late as 1944, parties of Chukchi were seen to arrive from Siberia on the Alaskan coast to hunt, fish, and trade, and American Eskimos visited Siberia on similar excursions. The Soviet Union, fearing such fraternization, increased its grip on the Chukchi area in a Sovietization program so that such interchange ended by the 1950s. American Eskimos at Little Diomede still pursue their ancient ivory carving arts, many of the craftsmen using the bow-and-mouth drill of their ancestors, and each summer they go to the mainland with their carvings to sell them in the main towns.

The arts and crafts of these and other Eskimos are preserved in a splendid museum at the University of Alaska in College, along with the creations of the Alaskan Indians. Ingenious and beautiful cradles, pots, knives, nets, and costumes give evidence of how a primitive people can still take time to ornament and give artistic significance to the most common tools.

Like the American Indian, the Eskimo supposedly is of Asiatic origin. A member of the Mongoloid peoples, he has a light brown skin, broad, flat face, and high cheekbones. Generally of short stature, his hair is black and straight.

Although the early Eskimos suffered much in conflict with or adjustment to white people's ways, they were generally left in possession of their lands. The arctic regions were not the kind to invite farmers or ranchers.

From 1848 on, increasing numbers of ships came to the arctic whaling grounds, bringing both good things and bad to the Eskimos. The ships' crews sought chiefly baleen, the long, flexible strips in the jaws of baleen whales through which such whales strain the shrimp, plankton, and other sea life they depend on for food. Baleen was in demand for such articles as stays for women's corsets and buttons. Also in demand was whale oil to be made into soap or candles. As the Eskimos learned to desire white men's goods, they eagerly awaited the arrival of the ships each spring to trade their stocks of baleen for guns, ammunition, and liquor.

Rum and whiskey were ruinous to many villages, but once the natives had experienced intoxication, many yearned for liquor above anything else. Unscrupulous whalers saw to it that their cargoes included a plentiful supply. The situation became so serious that in 1880 the United States tried to put a stop to the liquor traffic by assigning a revenue cutter to cruise the whaling grounds. By stealth, both whites and Eskimos continued the trade. At one Eskimo village, Point Hope, the natives refused to barter their baleen for anything except whiskey. There and elsewhere many learned how to make their own hooch out of a mash of flour and molasses left to ferment. In many a village the mash was as much a permanent fixture as the smoky seal oil lamp.

Permanent whaling stations, owned and operated by white men, were established along the Arctic coast. At these, whaling was done from shore, and Eskimos were hired to help during the whaling season, being paid with goods such as crackers, matches, rifles, tools, ammunition, and molasses. Along with goods came the deadly germs of smallpox and other diseases. Epidemics took a terrible toll of the Eskimo population. Many northern villages lost half of their numbers in a few years. To add to the Eskimos' troubles, the whale and seal herds were rapidly depleted. And many of the young hunters no longer knew how to use the old ways of hunting, having become dependent on rifles, for which often they lacked ammunition.

Missionaries began to arrive to Christianize and educate the natives. Schools and churches were built. Although many missionaries were sincerely dedicated to helping the native help himself, some had no appreciation of the basic culture or were extremely intolerant of certain of its forms. Ritual dances such as those attending the whaling season were discouraged by white religious sects that frowned on dancing of any kind. At Point Hope, missionaries burned down the dance halls where traditional dances were performed, partly to provide fuel, but mostly to destroy what they considered a pagan religion. The dances, performed by both men and women, were accompanied by male drummers. The Eskimo drum, a wooden hoop over which an animal membrane is stretched, is the Eskimo's only musical instrument. At certain other missions, as at Point Barrow, the missionaries urged the natives to abandon their snug quarters for frame houses. Such wooden houses were cold and drafty. While an igloo of the old style was snug, needing only an oil lamp to heat it, the frame shacks required stoves, and there was only driftwood to burn, and not much of that.

As Eskimos succumbed to modern ways, they found themselves increasingly in need of materials that were produced "outside"—flour, tea, fuel oil, guns, and eventually outboard motors and gasoline. A recent headline in an Alaskan native paper points up such dependence: KUSKOKWIM AREA VILLAGES GET EMERGENCY WINTER GASOLINE. The emergency shipment of three hundred barrels of gasoline had to be sent to villages in the Kuskokwim River delta area in response to a plea by residents who feared they would be unable to fuel their snowmobiles—commonly called "sno-gos" by the natives.

The end of commercial whaling, due to a diminishing market for whale products, came about 1915. This left most Eskimos in a dire situation. They had lost many of their own skills, had become dependent on the white man's goods and money, and at the same time found their natural resources vanishing, especially fur seals. An attempt to provide a new source of meat and hides was made by the United States Government as early as 1892, with the introduction of reindeer imported to Alaska from Siberia. The Bureau of Education, supervising this introduction of reindeer, brought herders from Siberia and Lapland to teach the Alaskan natives the proper methods of caring for the herds. In some ways the program was successful, but there were problems that worked against its being a real answer. The deer were easy victims for wolves or diseases, and if not carefully watched by herdsmen they tended to wander off with the native caribou. Some areas were overgrazed by careless herding. Mainly, the Eskimos of northwest Alaska are not herders. They tend to cling to their villages except when the cycle of whale or caribou hunting lures them away. So, while they were engaged in such hunting, many reindeer wandered off and were lost. In 1969, the reindeer program still continued on a small scale but predictions were that it would be officially terminated before long.

Though settlers of the kind who poured onto the more fertile lands of the Indians inhabiting what are known as the conterminous states—those having the same continental boundaries—did not make land claims on the Alaskan Arctic, there was another kind of fortune seeker who did. Such were the "stampeders," men who rushed north in hordes at the cry of "Gold!" The gold strike of 1896 in the Klondike region of Canada brought a stream of miners through Alaska. Then came the gold discoveries in Alaska itself—coastal Nome in 1899, interior Fairbanks in 1902. Miners and prospectors took over the land, setting up tent cities and shacks, brawling through regions new to white influence, staking out mining claims where formerly the natives had been the only tenants.

Alaska, then a territory, and now the largest of the states in the Union, with a combined area as large as Texas, California, and Montana put together, was still largely unknown in those days. Even after the gold rushes it remained so, though certain investigators began to realize the tremendous potentials there in minerals, timber, oil, and other natural resources.

World War II brought the greatest impact on Alaska from the "outside," as both natives and white Alaskans think of the forty-eight conterminous states. From the Aleutian Islands to Fairbanks to Barrow, military outposts and centers were constructed. At the latter place, today's largest Eskimo village in Alaska, the DEW Line (Distant Early Warning System) was built. Eskimos and Indians worked side by side with white workers from the Lower Forty-eight, and the process of acculturation —the taking on of traits from the dominant culture and the loss of culture identity by the weaker—was accelerated. Long before, Eskimo men and boys had ceased to put stones called labrets in their lower lips, as most women had abandoned the tattooing of their faces and bodies. But young girls were still imbued with a belief in the honor of courting males, this having been their experience with most Eskimo young men. They became easy prey to irresponsible young, white soldiers looking only for a good time. Young Eskimo or Indian men, driving tractors or motor sleds, accumulated cash money that they often spent on useless goods. Old ways were forgotten, even derided, and the dependence on outside support increased. Once the war was over and the military-based incomes decreased or disappeared, much of the native population was left in limbo. They could not go back successfully to ancient ways—having forgotten even what they were—but at the same time most lacked the education or skills to make their way in a competitive labor market in the cities of Juneau, Fairbanks, or Anchorage. Many could turn only to the government for help in the form of welfare checks.

The "swimming gold" of the fur otter was the beginning of the white invasion of Alaska, followed by the rush for mineral gold, and then the influx of American dollars during the Second World War. There was still another invasion to come. It arrived with the search for and discovery of "black gold" in the form of oil. Hope for oil discovery goes back as far as 1853 when oil seeps were observed. In 1923, a Point Barrow oil seep was put into a navy reserve covering thirty-seven thousand square miles of the Arctic Slope. Eventually, commercial companies became interested, and when one struck oil on the Kenai Peninsula, an oil rush pattern developed. In 1968, the "big bonanza" occurred when what was estimated as the greatest oil pool in history was discovered at Prudhoe Bay in the far north, an area of treeless tundra plain stretching southward from the Arctic Ocean to the north slope of the Brooks Mountain Range. In early July 1969, the state of Alaska opened bids submitted by representatives of the world's major oil companies who desired to lease the oil-rich land. This was the greatest competitive oil lease sale in United States' history and ended with the state treasury being richer by some $900 million. Whose land was being leased? Theirs, say the Eskimos, by right of prior occupancy and use, and they demand compensation for all lands taken from them.

Some native claims were filed over thirty years ago, but the majority were recorded in 1966–67. In December of 1966, Secretary of the Interior Stewart Udall halted action on the disposal of all public lands in the state to which natives claimed "aboriginal possession," basing his action on a congressional guarantee made in 1884 that Alaskan natives would not be disturbed in their use and occupancy of the lands. This land freeze was modified in January 1970 by Udall's successor, Walter Hickel, to forward work on the Trans Alaska Pipeline System.

Whatever the result of their land claims, both the natives and the land itself will be drastically disturbed. Conservationists are alarmed about the havoc that can be wrought in the "fragile" environment of the arctic wilderness. It takes many years for a thin cover of moss and lichen to grow on tundra where the subsoil is permanently frozen, a condition called permafrost. The thin, insulating cover can be quickly destroyed by tractor treads moving over it, the furrows left turning into watery canals to erode the soil. Further, there is the threat of oil leakage either from tankers or from the proposed forty-eight-inch-wide oil pipe to be built from Prudhoe Bay eight hundred miles south to Valdez. And with all this, there will be the intensified impact on the native peoples.

As against the millions of dollars the oil companies expect to make from their investments, the average income of Alaskan natives averages between $700 and $2000 a year. A current newspaper cartoon depicts an American Indian in a patched robe asking an Eskimo, oil derricks in the background, "Has the government assigned you your reservation yet?"

Alaska Chambers of Commerce and travel bureaus feature photographs of Eskimos dancing in colorful costumes, young natives studying at Bureau of Indian Affairs or in Headstart programs, high school bands and Boy Scout units. Less well publicized are pictures showing natives living in extreme stages of poverty. For the few who manage to live in modern houses, more live in dreary shacks or quonset huts, barely able to subsist on what they can earn or on what they receive from welfare checks.

The crux of the native problem is the need for education in order that people may be trained for jobs and professions. It is no longer sufficient for most to be a good hunter or maker of *mukluks;* the need today is to be able to speak and read English, run a typewriter or a bulldozer, study medicine or law, and fit into the overall white economy. For many years the Bureau of Indian Affairs has had the main responsibility for native welfare and has built many grammar schools in rural areas. Now, the state is trying to assume more of the responsibility. A great lack is high schools in the "bush," for without a high school education, young people are handicapped for jobs or for college. One attempt at a solution is that of sending grammar school graduates to boarding schools in cities. Youngsters may be sent to places such as Nome, Fairbanks, or Anchorage where they live with resident families while attending the high school available. Often, they are very far from their native villages, homesick and strange to city ways. When and if they become used to city patterns, they are apt to return to their home villages with a disdain of their parents' traditional ways. Girls in home economics class who have learned to use an electric stove are not apt to have much patience with a sputtering kerosene stove or one fueled by driftwood. Boys who have been trained to use a mechanical wood lathe are apt to scorn older whittling techniques. The parents, too, are troubled. Though they realize the need for their children to have a modern education, they dread their turning their backs on the old culture. What happens is that too few young persons manage to graduate from high school, not because of lack of ability but because of the conflicts and hardships involved. The majority go back to village life, frustrated and unhappy, or subsist in discontent on a low-paid job in the city.

Of the approximately fifty-five thousand native Alaskans, almost three quarters live in villages or small communities. In 1967, the BIA provided eighty-two schools, while sixty-three were operated by the state.

Education ends at the eighth grade in nearly all the villages, and only twenty-three schools in larger places offer ninth grade or above. Other schools are provided by missionaries.

Teachers, particularly non-native ones, do not have an easy job adjusting to the life in an Eskimo village with its usually primitive housing and its harsh weather. It is not easy to find well-trained teachers who will stay on the job, which includes the role of doctor or nurse as well as educator. Generally the most stable and sought after are husband-and-wife teams. Most needed of all are native teachers and native participants on school boards.

A very real difficulty in reaching the Eskimo student is that textbooks are usually oriented toward white, middle-class pupils. An Eskimo child for whom whale skin, *muktuk,* is considered a treat is not apt to be keenly interested in a textbook story dealing with a white child's treat of a hot dog. Or when a teacher asks, "Where do birds nest?" the child is not apt to have the expected answer. Instead of replying, "In the trees," the child will probably say, "On the ground," for the birds he knows in his treeless village are those who nest on shore. Some steps are being taken to try to relate books more to the Eskimo's own background.

Poverty and ill health are added factors. The native unemployment rate in 1969 was 60 per cent in the winter, 20 per cent in the summer. At a typical village, Nunapitchuk, visited by Senator Edward Kennedy in 1969 during a fact-finding tour by the United States Senate

Subcommittee on Indian Education, live four hundred natives. A family of eleven there lived in a tiny hovel in an area known as "Lousetown." Three beds, with dirty blankets, were crowded into the space, leaving barely room for an oil-burning stove used for both heat and cooking. The shack was lined with warped plywood or cardboard, both stained where melting snow had leaked. There were gaps in the walls, through which the strong winds blew except where snow had piled up to act as insulation. Under the snow were piles of garbage and even the bodies of dead dogs. Toilet facilities, as in most Eskimo houses, consisted of a pail.

In such an environment, disease quickly spreads. Tuberculosis has long been responsible for the high mortality rate of Eskimos. At Point Hope, which archeologists say is one of the oldest and largest continuously inhabited Eskimo villages, a study in 1956 showed that nearly 50 per cent of the population was affected by tuberculosis. But syphilis, once a very prevalent disease, had become non-existent. Influenza also takes a toll, as does measles. Many Eskimo babies still die of measles or whooping cough. Accidents, in 1969, were the greatest cause of mortality.

Most villages are without a resident doctor or hospital. The United States Public Health Service supplies school clinics with a limited amount of medical equipment for emergency situations. When a teacher or trader is in doubt as to how to treat a patient or accident victim, advice is sought and received by radio, a doctor answer-

ing questions on a special hookup. A United States Coast
Guard vessel makes yearly stops at villages to take X rays
and perform other medical services. And in some villages,
native women have formed health councils to try to help
people who are sick and assist visiting public health
teams.

The rural Eskimo villages have the highest birth
rate in the United States. Even so, the population levels
remain about the same because of the migration to cities.
The native villages are, in a sense, ghettos, but lacking
highways the only way out is by airplane, and airplane
tickets cost money. Yet, the determined and ambitious
manage, even though it is no simple matter for them to
adjust to city life with its noise, competition, and tempta-
tions. Even in Nome, which has a high percentage of
Eskimos, the rural refugee has difficulty adjusting, or
finding work.

According to the federal field committee for development planning in Alaska, the natives formerly lived
in "healthy poverty." Today they live in unhealthy
poverty, afflicted with many diseases, with a life expectancy half that of their white neighbors. Problems of
mental health are high on the list of their afflictions—
personality disorders rank third in incidence in the population. Acute brain syndrome, from intoxication, is the
eighth-ranked cause for hospitalization, and in the past sixteen years suicide has doubled.

The reservation termination plan evolved in the
1950s by the federal government applied to Eskimos as

well as the Indians of the Lower Forty-eight. Like the Indians, Eskimos were to be sent to industrial cities to become working citizens. In this relocation program, the brighter children were taken from their families, sent to boarding homes, and enrolled in the same schools as whites. To native parents, to missionaries, traders, doctors, and educators the drastic uprooting seemed to promise the extermination of the Indian and Eskimo races. Certainly it had a traumatic effect on many a young native transferred from a remote arctic village to the "foreign" climate of Chicago, Los Angeles, or Detroit.

In spite of the many obstacles, Eskimos are striving to meet their problems by themselves and have formed their own organizations to promote their welfare. For nearly fifty years the only organizations that existed were the Alaska Native Brotherhood and Sisterhood, the membership made up of Eskimos of southeastern Alaska. In 1961, northern Eskimos formed their own association. A need was felt for a group binding together all the native groups, and in 1966 the Alaska Federation of Natives (AFN)was formed. The AFN is in the vanguard of the fight to press native land claims. Beyond that, they are prepared to extend their influence into all social and economic areas affecting Alaska natives. Among their land claims attorneys is former Supreme Court Justice Arthur J. Goldberg, chief counsel for the organization. His partners are former Attorney General Ramsey Clark and former California Senator Thomas Kuechel. Originally, the natives submitted claims for approximately 290 million of Alaska's 375 million acres. They then reduced their claims to forty million acres, though asking $500 million in compensation over a nine-year period for lands previously lost, plus a 2 per cent royalty on the gross revenue of oil and gas leases made by the state and federal governments. They were encouraged by an earlier victory in which a group of Indians, the Tyoneks, won a claims settlement in the early 1960s. Lands awarded to the Tyoneks were leased by them to oil companies for bonuses of more than $30 million. Poverty stricken until then, the Tyoneks, located across Cook Inlet from Anchorage, became the Cinderellas of Alaska. The bulk of the money was entrusted to tribal leaders instead of to individuals and was used to improve the village or invested in Alaskan enterprises and statewide native undertakings.

As of late 1970, it appeared that the Alaskan natives would receive only a very small slice of the total Alaskan acreage inhabited by scattered bands of their forebears for thousands of centuries. In the summer of that year, the United States Senate voted to grant them only ten million acres—though the federal field committee reported that the natives require at least sixty million acres to subsist. The Senate offer also includes $1 billion in cash. The decision was by no means unanimous. Senator Fred Harris of Oklahoma urged a minimum of forty million acres, saying that the natives "own outstanding unextinguishable aboriginal title to approximately 93 per cent of the state of Alaska. Their claim rests not only on moral grounds, but also on firm legal grounds . . .

they live on the land. They are dependent on it for their livelihood." Senator Edward Kennedy, of Massachusetts, joined with Harris in his attitude.

The Arctic Slope Native Association also rejected the Senate proposal, as did almost every other native organization in the state. One of their elected spokesmen, Emil Notti, president of the AFN, said, "Our goal is not merely dollars and cents, but to give each native the opportunity to join the mainstream of American life on equal terms if that is his wish, or the opportunity to continue the traditional way of life while enjoying the full benefits of modern science, if that is his wish."

The government feels it is being generous in granting such reparations to the original owners of the land, even though it is over one hundred years since the United States purchased the area from Russia. Native ownership was ignored by both powers and no treaties were signed. If the House passes the Senate bill, all native claims in Alaska are to be wiped out. Though the settlement will clear the way for future technological development and increased economic prosperity for the state as a whole, including direct cash benefits to the natives, what will happen to their "traditional way of life" is that it will inevitably vanish.

Alaskan natives have their own weekly newspaper in the *Tundra Times,* edited in Fairbanks by Howard Rock, born in Point Hope. The paper legitimately proclaims itself the voice of the Eskimos, Aleuts, and Indians.

It also reports on the struggles of the Indians in the Lower Forty-eight, bringing attention to the latter's efforts to receive compensation for their own lost lands. Native pride is justifiably evident whenever a native achieves some recognition, as when a young National Guardsman in 1970 won the first Physical Combat Proficiency trophy ever won by a member of his race, or when a young woman becomes a college graduate. Many young native males enlist in the National Guard and they are proud of their record in World War II and their reputation as expert riflemen. As of December 1969, the *Times* reported that approximately four hundred veterans were attending college under the GI Bill—that electric power was to be extended to twenty-four remote villages so that by the end of 1970 nearly sixty communities would be so served, with a combined population of eighteen thousand persons. Even so, this is still a small part of the total native community.

The paper also publishes the darker side of native life, reminding readers that native life expectancy is roughly thirty-four years. The infant mortality rate is two-and-one-half times that of white Alaskans, and the per capita income is one fourth that of the whites.

There are other native voices finding expression, one of the most enterprising being a little, mimeographed sheet put out by the school children of tiny Arctic Village far up in the northern interior. Though the paper is called *Arctic Village Echoes,* there are very few echoes of an ancient culture in its pages. The children or adult contributors write chiefly of the arrival of the mail plane, the prospect of turkey at Thanksgiving, the visit of an air-borne Santa Claus from the air force base in Anchorage, the need for parts to make their "sno-gos" function. The Midnight Sun Native Store advertises its wares: "English Muffins, Peanut Butter (crunchy), Chicken Noodle Soup—Tang, Grapefruit, Corn and many other items on order." Thus have today's Alaskan Indians changed.

Yet, the coming of the caribou in the fall remains an exciting occasion, and the crude drawings of the children reveal the drama of the hunt. In the late November 1969 issue of *Echoes,* the youngsters' brief news notes repeated over and over that caribou had been sighted. Typical is the report, "The airplane came yesterday. The pilot saw caribou from the airplane. The caribou is coming toward the village. We get meat from the caribou. It is good for me to eat it. I am happy now. My father will shoot caribou. I like caribou." Another adds, "If the caribou come, I will eat boiled meat and fried meat. I am getting tired of fish and chicken. Everybody don't have meat right now. So they buy lots of canned meat."

The catch of a whale, the killing of caribou still are a time for festivity in Alaskan native villages, even though today the animals are hunted by motorboats or snowmobiles. But life is drastically changed, as the older natives appreciate. From the same little Arctic Village paper comes the reminiscences of an adult, written in the groping grammar and spelling characteristic of most in the villages. "The old days we all use a dog team to get logs, food and travel across country. Also live in tent all year around, no home. So wherever we set up the tent that's our home. About clothing we used to make our own out of caribou and canvas. Didn't use no money at all. Today we all got to have money even to get things. When we need things all we do is order it and get it the next mail day. . . . The other day I went to get firewood with the sno-go which is six miles out. It took me forty-five minutes out and back. It used to take me four hours on that trip."

The "generation gap" is worldwide. While older Eskimos at the main villages perform their ancient dances for the tourists, the younger generation watches from the sidelines, torn between interest, amusement, or disdain. Many young men seldom wear Eskimo clothing except when hunting, and even then they are more apt to wear National Guard parkas and boots that are not nearly as adequate as the old-style garments. Girls, too, prefer American clothes, their ideas of fashion coming from the mail-order catalogues, the chief "shopping center" for remote villagers. Home permanent waves are popular.

It is hard for the younger and older people to communicate, especially if the older people cling to "out-moded" ways. In the past, older people were respected for their accumulated knowledge, and were considered figures of authority. Today, the older individual is a power chiefly because of his or her old-age assistance check. The *money* is respected even if its recipient is not. Once mighty hunters or sewers of skin clothing now find themselves brushed aside as authorities.

Formerly, the elders taught the young men the lore of hunting in the ceremonial house, but the pattern has been broken. Highly organized ceremonial organizations that once provided social status and stability are largely forgotten. Marriages between young persons were once arranged by adults, but not in an inflexible way. Today's young natives are imbued with the idea of romantic love. At Fairbanks' Alaskaland, a commercial show place built to re-create the times of the early natives and stampeders, Eskimo ice cream made from whipped seal oil is a tourist offering. The Eskimos themselves prefer a modern sundae or a Cola float.

A most popular spot in the native village of Kotzebue is Bonnie's Bubble Room where one of the first coin-operated laundromats north of the Arctic Circle was installed. Children, especially, are fascinated. Whether wearing parkas or Montgomery Ward clothes, they like to stand and watch the lights flash on and off while the laundry spins around behind the glass doors. And there, they have the additional pleasure—if they have the money —of pushing the buttons on a candy, Coke, and sandwich vending machine.

Although some natives are aware of the values they have lost and try to keep ancient arts alive with the help of cooperative craft associations, increasing numbers feel the need to become a functioning part of the white society. They want to remain Eskimos or Indians but they also want to share in the benefits of contemporary society. In most villages, dog sled teams remain but only as an adjunct to the snowmobile, there being times when there is not enough snow for the latter or the machine breaks down in freezing cold. The silent *kayak* is being replaced by the noisy, outboard motorboat. For those adrift in the cities, the bar too often replaces the tribal council as a meeting place.

And now the oil derricks and pipelines are moving in, cutting a mighty track across the heart of Alaska. The success of Humble Oil Company's huge, ice-breaking tanker crunching its way through the Northwest Passage to Alaska's oil rich North Slope, in 1969, has opened the way to further traffic across the Top of the World. Towns such as Fairbanks and the port of Valdez are on their way to becoming boom towns, as during gold-rush days. The natives of the bare tundra, like those of the coast in whaling days, will feel the full impact of white technology and attitudes. For the many who are poorly educated, ill housed, this will be a wrenching experience.

At the Twentieth Alaska Science Conference held at the University of Alaska in August 1969, one of the important panel discussions was "The Condition of Alaskan Natives Today." In the three days of the conference, only one native was included in any of the meetings. A young Yukon Indian asked why there was no more than one native voice on a subject so vital to Eskimo, Aleut, or Indian. The reply was that no native was adequately qualified to appear with the white specialists and scholars. Natives could argue that statement, pointing to those among them who have been elected to public office or have become teachers, artists, pilots, and skilled mechanics. But if the statement is true, then it emphasizes the urgency to prepare the native population far better than has been the case in the past.

The culture and hunting methods of the aboriginal Canadian Eskimos were similar to those of the Alaskan Eskimos. Eskimos in Canada continued in old ways—hunting, fishing, trapping—until increasing contact with fur trader and missionary began to affect their lives drastically around 1950. Certain groups suffered extremely in the culture conflict. The population decreased alarmingly from disease, famine, and destitution, the decline in game animals being a major factor. Concerned persons, private and official, brought the Canadian Eskimo's plight to attention, and the Canadian government began a massive policy of relief. Basically, the policy stated that hunting and trapping could no longer provide these natives with their basic requirements and that government welfare assistance should be funneled into the Eskimo community. By 1965, hunting and trapping as a means of livelihood had all but disappeared, so that now most Eskimo families in Canada live in government-staffed villages along the Arctic shore.

This "disappearance" of the Canadian-dwelling Eskimo had begun long before. In the 1920s, when the Danish explorer Knud Rasmussen traveled across the icy wastes of northern Canada, guns had already begun to replace bows and arrows. Today even the traditional snow igloos have gone. As in Alaska, cargo planes fly over the vanishing dog sled trails, carrying lumber for frame houses and factory-made clothing for trading posts. The ancient charms and amulets such as owl claws are gone. The magic chants and special songs for strength and good luck are mostly forgotten. When the Christian missionaries first came to Eskimo centers in the far North, the native hunters substituted pages torn from the Bible as sacred charms when they started out on their hunts. Today, they say simple Christian prayers.

Whether Alaskan, Canadian, Greenland, or Siberian Eskimos, all are closely related racially and culturally, speaking variations of the same language. And their aspirations are generally the same—to become a productive and sharing part of the modern world. With any kind of chance, the Alaskan Eskimo, especially, can contribute much to that world. It remains to be seen if Congress will give this persevering and able people the opportunity and the justice denied for so long to other native Americans.

3.
Volcanoes
and
Surf

HAWAIIANS

For many weeks, in the fall of 1778, the natives of the Hawaiian Islands had watched the two strange ships sailing along their coasts. The three-masted vessels were larger than even the largest of their hollowed-log canoes in which they could carry fifty or more passengers along with cargo. These visiting ships were so huge that it seemed they could not have been made by ordinary men. They must be floating islands, a creation of the gods. More, the square-rigged sails hanging from the cross spars resembled the bark cloth banners that hung from the carved image of the god Lono that the islanders carried in their harvest ceremonies. It could only mean that Lono himself was a passenger and had come from his distant, dim abode to visit them in the flesh.

On the largest of the eight islands, Hawaii, run-

ners sped from one village to another, carrying news of
every movement of the ships. Nobles and commoners
shared in the excitement and all began feverish prepara-
tions for the great day of Lono's arrival. The high chiefs
got ready their brilliant robes and helmets made of bird
feathers, while the cooks prepared for a lavish feast,
which along with their staples of poi, yams, breadfruit,
and bananas must include such delicacies as roast pig
and dog.

Lono, the priests said, would put in at Kealakekua Bay, the Pathway of the Gods. So it was there
that people began to gather, first by the hundreds, then
by the thousands. Some came by canoe while others
traveled on foot, or in the case of chiefs were carried on
the backs of their servants. All babbled about the two
ships and the strangers that manned them. Some of the
islanders had visited the ships when they anchored offshore at other parts of the island. The strangers had
white skins, they reported, and openings in the sides
of their bodies into which they could push their hands
and draw out wondrous things such as nails or beads
in exchange for food from the islanders. New arrivals
brought the information that the floating islands had
rounded the South Cape and were now heading northward
toward the Pathway of the Gods, just as the priests had
predicted. By the time the foreign ships came in sight,
the rocky shore, the trees, the grass roofs of the houses,
and the surrounding hills were crowded with people.
Groups of women, naked except for grass skirts, leaped

and clapped their hands in a dance accompanied by shrill chants.

On board the ships, the men with the white skins looked across the harbor, amazed at the throngs. The ships were the *Resolution* and the *Discovery*, both stout vessels from England sent out under Captain James Cook, who had previously surveyed the coasts of Newfoundland and Labrador and then those of New Zealand and eastern Australia. Further, he had sailed around the globe, explored the Antarctic Ocean, and discovered a number of new lands. This was not the first time he had visited the islands to which he gave the name Sandwich Islands in honor of his patron, the Earl of Sandwich. At the very beginning of 1778, he had discovered the islands of Oahu, Kauai, and Niihau, part of the Hawaiian chain. At Kauai he had his first direct meeting with the islanders who swarmed the decks of the ships, bringing from their loaded canoes everything from fish to seashells. Even though they had never seen white men before, they eagerly bartered their produce for nails and scraps of iron, and the first experiment in trade had been a friendly one.

Now, ten months later, after having sailed up the northwest coast of America in a vain search for a Northwest Passage, a navigable strait across the top of North America, Cook had retreated from the Arctic back to the Sandwich Islands. He had found further islands in the chain, Molokai and Maui, and finally this largest one with its mighty volcanoes rearing up over lava-strewn coasts, brilliant bays, palms, and spuming waterfalls.

For six weeks he and his men had sailed around the island of Hawaii, surveying the coast, fighting stormy weather, and searching for a safe harbor. Now, on January 17, he ordered the anchors dropped in Kealakekua Bay. Even before the anchors plunged, fleets of native canoes surrounded the two ships. Cook wrote in his journal that there were at least twenty-five hundred canoes, each carrying an average of six persons. He estimated that "there were at least 15,000 men, women and children in the canoes, besides those that were on floats, swimming without floats, and actually on board and hanging round the outside of the ships."

He ordered a light boat lowered, invited two chiefs who appeared to be of highest rank to join him in the boat, and then was rowed ashore by his barge crew. Chanting, shouting, splashing islanders surrounded him and when he reached the beach, the two chiefs walked ahead of him, waving tall white poles from side to side, proclaiming, "Lono is with us. Make way. The great Lono is here." The people fell back, covered their faces, and spread themselves on the ground. Other chiefs joined the first two, leading Cook through masses of brown bodies toward an elaborate temple. The commoners edged back; only high priests were permitted within the chamber. There, Cook permitted himself to be anointed with coconut oil, listened to prayers and incantations, and was finally seated with his lieutenants at a sumptuous feast—complete with a priest prepared to chew his food for him.

Cook took advantage of his godly status and the willing help of the Hawaiians to repair and replenish his ships. The natives worked enthusiastically, filling the ships' water casks, hauling in pork, fruit, and vegetables for the reward of a few nails and bits of iron. The greatest reward was the spear points, daggers, and fish hooks the ship's blacksmith made for them. For aside from scraps of nails or metal that appeared in driftwood that washed ashore, the islanders were unfamiliar with metal. Their tools were mainly sharpened sticks for digging holes necessary to planting, axes made of stone for hollowing out their log canoes, knives of shark's teeth, awls and scrapers from shells. They did know how to make fire, rubbing a slender stick back and forth in a groove on a softer piece of wood until the friction produced heat to ignite a dry piece of bark cloth.

All went well during the English party's stay and on January 25 the king of the island, who had been absent on Maui, returned. With much ritual, the king welcomed Cook, exchanged names with him, gave him several feather cloaks and a supply of hogs, sugar cane, and other goods. Cook, in return, gave King Kalaniopuu a linen shirt and his own cutlass. Meanwhile, the scientists with Cook carried out their explorations and studies.

Finally, all was ready and it was time to leave. Although there had been misunderstandings, and the islanders had been drained of supplies, there was no hint of trouble. On February 4, Cook and his crews sailed north. They were barely beyond sight of the towering volcano, Mauna Loa, when tempest winds struck. Four days later, the winds became a typhoon slashing the sails of the *Discovery* and breaking the foremast of the *Resolution*. There was nothing to do but struggle back to Kealakekua Bay.

Cook's reception this time was very different from before. Not a single canoe appeared to greet him, and the villages were mostly deserted. In the expressions of those villagers who did come forward there was skepticism and even hostility. What kind of a super being was Cook if he could not control the weather but must come limping back to port with his floating islands battered?

At anchor, the crews worked to repair the ships. Some of the natives paddled close by, menacingly flourishing the daggers they had been given. Worse, some of the ships' valuable articles were stolen. There were bouts of violence as the islanders became increasingly bold. Then, one morning, it was found that a cutter anchored off the *Discovery*'s bow had been stolen in the night. Cook could not spare the cutter. Leading an armed group of marines ashore he planned to seize the king, take him on ship and hold him as a hostage until the cutter was returned.

At first, it seemed he would succeed, but the aroused villagers gathered around, brandishing clubs, spears, and their new iron daggers. Cook attempted to retreat. In the impending melee, he was separated from his companions who, terrified, had jumped into the water and waded toward the boat that had brought them from the ship. Cook turned his back on the howling natives, shouting orders to the retreating crew. A club landed and he sprawled face downward in the water. He tried to rise. A dagger ripped into his back. At once, hordes of natives swarmed around him. Lono was dead. Even though he had not proved to be superhuman, they were still not certain that he was simply a mortal, and so they treated his remains as they did those of royalty. They divided his body into many pieces and gave a piece to each high priest around the countryside.

After a series of bloody skirmishes between the English and the islanders, there was a truce during which the English managed to recover most of Cook's bones, and the needed equipment on shore, but the valued cutter had been taken apart for its nails. Under a new commander, the *Discovery* and *Resolution* set sail, never to return to Hawaii. Not until six years later did any other whites intrude on the islands' isolation. This was not because of fear of the natives but simply because the islands were all but unknown and hard to find, mere dots in the huge Pacific Ocean, thousands of miles from the European ports or those of the newly formed United States.

Yet, the Hawaiian Islands had been colonized centuries before. The colonizers were dwellers of the South and Central Pacific. They were called Polynesians, from the Greek, meaning many islands. For reasons or circumstances no one can be sure of, whole families left their homelands of Tahiti, Samoa, the Marquesas, and other islands. In their large canoes they roamed thousands of miles across the uncharted waters. They had only the stars, the steady trade winds, migration patterns of birds, the waves and currents to guide them. They used sails of woven coconut or pandanus fiber and as many as a hundred men in double canoes paddled, bailed, and trimmed the sails. Tucked into the hulls and deckhouses were water and food to sustain them; additional food could be taken from the sea. It appears that these South Sea "Vikings" first sighted the Hawaiian Islands around the eleventh century.

The islands were not altogether the lush, palm-tree-stippled land spots pictured in travel posters today though they were fertile and inviting. Then, as now, they were young islands created by volcanic activity, and though there were forests in uplands and valleys, and some greenery on shore, there were broad stretches of desert and bare lava with no animals except birds, insects, and sea life. The climate was temperate, though, and the soil seemed right for producing plants such as sweet potatoes, breadfruit, coconuts, and bamboo. Skilled in agriculture, the Polynesians planted cuttings of coco palm, banana, and breadfruit trees they had brought with them, and built their grass huts, attempting to create their society on the patterns they had used in their former island homes. They also brought dogs, pigs, and chickens.

There was sporadic, perhaps accidental traffic between Hawaii and the settlers' original island homes even though these, such as Tahiti, could be some twenty-five hundred miles distant. Then, gradually, such visits diminished, and finally ceased. For some centuries before Captain Cook arrived, the Hawaiian settlers were isolated, their only knowledge of the world beyond being what was passed down through spoken legends and songs from one generation to the next. The population grew, different regions being governed by warrior chiefs. Chiefs fought each other to increase the size of their kingdoms, and the larger islands—Hawaii, Maui, Oahu, and Kauai—were often ruled by families of chiefs. The kings were all powerful, owning all the land, holding the power of life and death over their subjects. Under an island king were the chiefs of royal blood; the priests, among whom were astronomers, prophets, teachers; the masses, the great majority who did the main labor; and the slaves, a small group whose ancestors had been slaves, as they were doomed to be. Since royalty was hereditary, it meant that women as well as men could be in high position. Hawaii's last ruler, 1893, was Queen Liliuokalani.

It was essentially a feudal society like that in Europe during the Middle Ages, and the lot of the commoner depended on the character of the king and head chiefs. The only beings higher than the king were the large number of Hawaiian gods, for theirs was a polytheistic religion. Some gods, like Lono, were good and helpful if one presented them with the proper gifts; others, like Pele who had her abode in the fiery cone of Kilauea, were treacherous and sinister. A special group of priests spent their time trying to gain Pele's favor, pitching thousands of hogs, valuable goods, and even human sacrifices in the form of unlucky commoners into the volcano's scalding crater. Each Hawaiian family had an ancestral guardian spirit and its image was treated as a living thing needing daily attention, even to sharing one's food with it. Not to place a bit of breadfruit or a choice piece of fried octopus before its shrine regularly could bring disaster. All Hawaiians, from king to slave, worshiped four Polynesian gods above all others. These were Kane, father of life and light; Ku, the god of war who demanded human sacrifices; Kaneloa, ruler of the land of departed spirits; Lono, the god of growing things, sports, and peace. Public worship was held in temples decorated by large, carved images of the gods, with rites on certain days of the month. Along with gods, the islanders peopled the rocks, trees, and waves with ghosts, elves, and demons. No Hawaiian, whether he simply planned to mash taro root on a board to make poi or was setting out to fish, ever began any activity without chanting a prayer or performing a religious rite. At the same time, he was careful to use his considerable practical skills, fully aware of their value.

In social conduct, the great regulator was the *kapu* system, the word being a variant of the Polynesian "tabu," or our word "taboo." Anything *kapu* was forbidden. To violate a *kapu* was to risk the vengeance of the supernatural powers. DO NOT TOUCH! To do so could set off a chain of events that could destroy the world.

There were numberless *kapus* pertaining to all activities—eating, working, playing—and some were seasonal or temporal, while others were permanent. It was unthinkable, for instance, that men and women should eat together, and so a family required several buildings: a men's eating house and one for the women; a chapel for the male's private worship; a woman's workroom where she could make tapa cloth or other needed articles; a general storage house for tools, canoes, or surfboards; and a central structure like a "family room" where the family could sleep, chat, or entertain. Men had to be their own cooks. *Kapus* also governed what could be eaten; pork, bananas, coconuts, and some kinds of fish were forbidden to women. Food was boiled by dropping hot stones into a calabash of water, but chiefly food was baked in an oven dug into the earth.

The houses were constructed of wood frames lashed together with cords made from rootlets and vines, then thatched with various grasses or leaves tied in bundles. If rocks were available, the lower part of the house was usually of stone. If the dwelling stood where floods threatened, it was built on stilts. Although Cook complained that the island villages looked like disorderly collections of haystacks, the structures were resilient in the face of the strong trade winds and, with some patching, could last for years.

The common picture of Hawaiians offered by

Hollywood has been that of a people largely engaged in doing nothing but singing, making leis of flowers for necklaces or headbands, playing ukuleles and Hawaiian guitars, and dancing the hula. The Hawaiians of the past had neither the ukulele or the guitar—these were inventions of white immigrants. The instruments they did have were primitive wind instruments, rattles, a crude stringed bow that gave out a twang when plucked, and various kinds of drums. Singing was limited to a range of perhaps five or six notes.

It is true that they enjoyed sports and festivals when there was time for these, but the major part of the year they had to work very hard to provide for themselves and for the royalty that lived off their labors. Everything needed for building had to be lugged by hand for they had no wheeled vehicles and no draft animals. Work in the fields was arduous, sometimes in stifling dust, sometimes in waist-deep mud. Weather varied according to region. Some crops were raised on the moist, grassy uplands, others in the lowlands where it was necessary to terrace the fields and bring water to them by irrigation ditches. Here, again, the human body was the chief tool, the bottoms of such ditches being firmed by the people joining together in a mass and rhythmically stamping their feet in unison, chanting to keep time. Or, in bringing rocks to a construction site, men would form a long line and heave the boulders from one to another. The sea provided an abundance of sea food but often the waves were turbulent, offering a challenge even to such excellent seafarers.

And there were always the smaller daily routines —the dogs and pigs in their pens had to be fed, fresh water or salt water had to be carried from often distant sources, firewood for the outdoor ovens chopped by a stone ax. In spite of all this, the people were generally contented and were lavish with their gifts of produce. Above them were the kings and chiefs who lived in luxury, served by a vast assortment of servants and attended by harems of wives. So long as such rulers were not too despotic, the people did not complain.

There is some basis in fact for the Hollywood stereotype of the frolicking native, distorted though it is, and that is when the harvest moon of October arrived, work ceased. So did wars. This was the *Makahiki* season, the Hawaiian Christmas, Fourth of July, and Thanksgiving rolled into one. For those who could afford it, the celebration lasted for three to four months, during which time the emphasis was on games, sport, merrymaking, pageants, and surfing.

The Hawaiians were masters at riding the waves on their specially built boards, excelling all the surfers of eastern Polynesia. They rode the boards prone, kneeling, or standing up, men, women, and children joining in the sport. A lieutenant with Cook wrote, "The boldness and address with which I saw them perform these difficult and dangerous maneuvers was altogether astonishing and is scarcely to be believed." On a day of good surf conditions, even though it might not be during *Makahiki,* an entire community would take to the spuming, white water, royalty on surfboards, commoners body surfing. When the ocean was still, offering no rolling swells, surfers would wade in carrying strands of beach morning glory, strike the water with the plants, and recite a chant pleading with the ocean to well up.

Like almost everything else, surfing had its sacred aspect, requiring rituals from the felling of a tree for the surfboard to its final construction. In the way that the New England Indian planted a fish with his corn hills, the islander placed a fish, with a prayer, in the roots of the felled tree as a religious offering. In both cases, the ritual contributed fertilizer to enrich the soil. Special surfboards were reserved for the nobles, and chiefs competed with each other in surfing contests.

Along with surfing during the long celebration of harvest were contests at running, wrestling, javelin throwing, canoe riding, and dart tossing. In the long, mild evenings, simple games and gambling provided entertainment, and a pastime called *ume* in which chosen male and female partners withdrew from the group to spend an hour alone. The Hawaiians considered sexual relations as much an ordinary part of life as eating or breathing, though governed by definite rules, especially after puberty. They were by no means licentious, as the missionaries mistakenly assumed, being confused by the children calling all aunts "mother," and all uncles "father."

Hula performances were an essential part of *Makahiki,* and these dances were not simply a swaying of the hips by grass-skirted young women. Male and female, young and old, participated in the dance, which involved the manipulation of arms, feet, hands, hips, and torso, each gesture having a symbolic significance. There were serious and comic forms of hula, vigorous and restrained. The hula was part of the Hawaiian vocabulary.

The climate did not require much in the way of clothing. Tattooing was often enough in the way of decoration, though the men did wear a loin strap called *malo,* the women a short-skirted *pau.* Even if these were missing there was no embarrassment. Either sex might wear a square shawl in the evening to ward off a cool breeze or rain. Lacking looms, the women made bed-covers and costumes from the inner bark of the paper mulberry tree. This was peeled off, soaked, scraped, and beaten into thin strips. The strips were overlapped to increase the width of the material, and built up into layers for thickness. Beaten with a mallet on a wooden anvil, this became tapa and was decorated. Leatherwork was done with much skill. Most remarkable were the cloaks and helmets made from the tufts of small birds. Specialized bird catchers went into the forests and trapped the wanted birds on twigs smeared with a sticky substance, or in nets. The Hawaiians did not kill the birds but pulled only a few of the colorful feathers, then released the birds to grow new ones.

Some historians speculate that earlier ships, perhaps Spanish, may have visited the Hawaiian Islands
before Captain Cook. If so, they left no definite traces.
Cook, in spite of his attempts to keep his crew from
fraternizing with the native women—who were willing
enough to invite the sailors to their grass huts—left behind
him the infection he wanted to avoid, venereal disease.
And so, with his arrival in the islands, the white man's
imprint was indelibly made.

More *haole* were to come, *haole* being the name
that Hawaiians applied to all outsiders whether black,
yellow, or white, though in time it came to mean white
only. Beginning around 1785, British and then American
fur traders carrying pelts from the Northwest Coast to
trade in China began pausing at the islands for supplies
on their way back and forth. Some of the visiting captains
managed to persuade a few natives to join them on their
journey homeward, to display them to the people back
home. Or they hired them as crew members. The usual
fate was that the transplanted Hawaiians found themselves stranded in London, New England, Canton, or
other foreign places, once public interest in their novelty
waned. So many Hawaiians were stranded in New England in the 1800s that a mission school was started at
Cornwall, Connecticut, to train them, American Indians,
and others who might serve as translators for missionaries
going to spread Christianity among their peoples.

To most of the fur traders and the whalers
after them, the islanders were pagan savages. Interested

in profits, these traders tried to outwit the chiefs and kings, while the latter usually parried in kind. A few whites, impressed by the temperate climate or tempted by commercial possibilities, "went native" to the extent that they settled permanently in these almost virginal lands. Foreigners were generally welcomed by the Hawaiians and it became the fashion for each chief to have at least one white as an adviser. In 1794, there were around a dozen foreigners settled in Hawaii, including American, English, Irish, and Chinese. The foreign "invasion" increased until twenty-five years later there were perhaps as many as two hundred permanent settlers.

One of the earlier and most important visitors was the English captain, George Vancouver, who first stopped in the islands in the spring of 1792. This was during the reign of Kamehameha I, the young ruler of the northern end of Hawaii, the "Big Island." Vancouver became well acquainted with the people and especially with the young king who was interested in promoting trade with the whites. On Vancouver's second visit to the island he brought longhorn cattle and sheep with him. When Kamehameha first saw the cattle he feared the "big hogs" would attack him, and when a cow ran amuck on the beach, the Hawaiians fled in panic. The offspring of these and later, better breeds of cattle eventually became the base of Hawaii's cattle industry. Mexican *vaqueros,* or cowboys, were imported to teach the islanders the arts of cattle handling. Vancouver also brought in goats and geese, and gave orange and almond trees to the chiefs of the various islands. In time, oranges became an important island product for export.

Kamehameha had a dream of uniting the islands into one kingdom, and succeeded. He was ruthless in war but once the fighting was over he was a good statesman, especially eager to advance his own welfare and his kingdom through commerce. "He wants all he sees," one commentator said. His subjects, too, wanted the white man's goods and many swapped whatever they had for tools, guns, and whiskey, favoring the new intoxicant over their extra-potent native brew, *kava*. Kamehameha himself became addicted to the white man's liquor for a time, always keeping a flask handy, but when he saw what problems resulted from drunkenness among his people, he limited himself and finally gave such liquor up entirely and prohibited its being made in his kingdom.

Among the whites who settled in the islands were ship deserters, convicts, or unprincipled opportunists. Some of these abused and robbed the natives and helped to corrupt the young women of the villages. Other, more responsible persons, retired captains or common seamen set up shops and started businesses. Although, compared to later times, the time under Kamehameha was a golden age, the basic structures of the islanders' society were being steadily undermined. People who had given freely of whatever goods they had began to understand the principle of profit from exchange. Imitating the ways of the whites, they learned to drive hard bargains. No longer would they exchange a pig for one or two nails.

Now they wanted chisels, saws, cloth, guns, ammunition, and more and more rum.

Though the commoners had always needed to work hard, there had been the reward of working together in a common purpose for tangible goods. Then came the sandalwood trade. Sandalwood, much valued by China for incense, idols, and fancy boxes grew wild in Hawaii. The king saw a chance to become an exporter in a big way. Since the land belonged to him, he ordered his chiefs to see to it that the people spent their time cutting down sandalwood trees, regardless of the season or their other duties. And so the commoners went out into the hills, seeking the precious wood, cutting it into lengths they could carry on their backs, groaning over distances of ten to thirty miles to transport it. Doomed to such labor, their fields and fishing canoes lay idle, and even the sacred celebrations of the *Makahiki* were abandoned. As the sandalwood on lower hills gave out they had to climb ever higher for the trees, which they began to hate. Above, they shivered in chilling rains, without proper shelter; below, their families suffered in the neglected grass huts. After the death of Kamehameha in 1819 (the year the first whale was killed in Hawaiian waters) the sandalwood business continued with vigor under his successor. Men and women strapped six-foot logs to their backs and climbed between the woods and the measuring pits by day and by night. In the cold weather, on Kauai in 1830, they were driven by hunger to eat moss. This massive exploitation of the common people—which benefited mostly the traders, chiefly American—contributed to a gradual decline in the native population. Thousands died of famine or from plagues that swept through the villages.

In time, the sandalwood forests were nearly destroyed, as was the aboriginal Hawaiian culture. Exposed to the contradictions and contributions of the white man's culture, which included the introduction of the rat, the mosquito, flea, and cockroach, the islanders became dispirited, their belief in the old ways and gods undermined. Before his death, Kamehameha had realized that the faith of his subjects was wavering, and begged, "Be loyal to the gods and all will be well with you."

So far had the ancient beliefs crumbled that the new king Kamehameha II, or Liholiho, realized that it was impossible to retain the *kapu* system in the face of encroaching white civilization. Urged on by influential women among his advisers, particularly Kaahumanu, widow of the dead king, he ordered a public banquet. There, for the first time in the islands' history, he and other men sat down and ate openly with women. The goddess Pele did not cause Mauna Loa to spout fiery death over the islands, nor did the gods of the deep send waves crashing over the shores. Nothing at all happened except that after the quiet meal, the young king ordered that all the old temples should be destroyed and the idols chopped to pieces. There was some open resistance among opponents of the drastic order and some bloodshed, but the ancient gods of the Hawaiians were doomed and were thereafter worshiped only in secret by the faithful. For most, the release from the taboos left them in limbo.

This shattering of ancient beliefs was wonderful news to New England Christian missionaries who only a few months later landed on the islands to bring their own religion to the natives. The team of missionaries was composed of seven married couples under the leadership of the Reverend Hiram Bingham. They were accompanied by four young Sandwich Islanders who had been rescued from destitution and educated at the school in Cornwall. Now the young converts were to serve as translators and as witnesses to the desirability of having missions in Hawaii.

When the missionaries approached the harbor in the spring of 1820, they did not know whether they would confront a storm of arrows or be seized and put into a pot to boil—though Hawaiians were never cannibals. The travelers had already suffered much on the eighteen-thousand-mile journey around the tip of South America, miserable in the rough quarters of the trade ship, racked by seasickness and fear of what lay ahead. And now, through their spyglasses, they could see the pagans on shore, and then the canoes slicing toward them through the water.

The natives had no knowledge of the special group of passengers but rowed out to meet the vessel at the northern tip of Hawaii as they always did when a trade ship appeared. The missionaries were not reassured by their first sight of the islanders. To the Reverend Bingham "the appearance of degradation and barbarism among the chattering, almost naked natives was appalling. Some of our number with gushing tears turned away from the spectacle. Others with firmer nerves continued their gaze, but were ready to exclaim, 'Can these be human beings! How dark and comfortless their state of mind and heart! How imminent the danger of the immortal soul! . . . Can we throw ourselves upon these rude shores, and take up our abode for life among such people for the purpose of training them for heaven?'"

Bingham and his dedicated colleagues were in for a pleasant surprise when the ship anchored in the bay at Kawaihae. There they learned that the king himself had banished the old idols and declared the end of the *kapu* system. The islands were ripe for new sanctions, since their idols had been destroyed, and the natives greeted the little band of Christians with cheers, bringing on board canoe loads of gifts. However, though Liholiho had struck at the heart of the islands' own religion, he was not enthusiastic about having the white strangers settle down to introduce a new faith. After much debate, he finally agreed to let the New Englanders stay for one year, on trial.

Except for wives of sea captains, the missionary ladies were the first white women the natives had ever seen, and their curiosity was boundless. From the houses, taverns, and coconut groves of Honolulu, the Hawaiians stared at the long gowns, the poke bonnets, the high, laced shoes. Very soon, the native women would be wearing dresses of the same kind, the *holoku*, or Hawaiian Mother Hubbard gown, created by the missionary wives. Soon, too, they would be learning the new religion which, in some ways, with its "Thou shalt nots" seemed to have as many *kapus* as the religion they had begun to discard. Aside from the Bible's ten commandments, the pious Protestant missionaries had many other negative commands against dancing, gambling, nudity, theatricals, freegoing sexual relations, and drinking or smoking. Even so, the islanders flocked to hear the missionaries give their sermons in halting Hawaiian. By the end of their first year, the missionaries had about one hundred pupils of both sexes and all ages in the schools they established at various locations to teach the meaning of Christianity. Their pupils were mainly adult and of high rank. Although some tavern owners and other elements who much preferred the old way of things were anti-missionary, Liholiho granted the Christian teachers permission to stay on indefinitely.

Within eight years, the Reverend Bingham was preaching in a pole-and-thatch tabernacle in Honolulu to congregations of two thousand natives. On the Big Island, another minister's congregations were so huge that the packed groups of natives, men on one side, women on the other, could only find sitting space by all sitting down at the same moment at a signal. The turn toward Christianity had been greatly helped by the dowager queen, Kaahumanu, who had influenced Liholiho in the destruction of the *kapu* system. Powerful politically, she was also imposing physically, being six feet tall and weighing over three hundred pounds. In 1824, she took the lead in urging Christianization of the realm.

Fatness was considered a mark of beauty by the Hawaiians. When Queen Kaahumanu (the name means "feather cloak") attended religious services she often rode in a small, American-built wagon, her great weight hauled by six servants. Another high-ranking native woman, Kapiolani, dramatically gave evidence of her conversion. She led a hundred-mile march to the steaming pit of Kilauea. There she defied the ancient and fierce goddess Pele. Tradition decreed that any visitor to the bubbling crater must tear off a branch of berries and throw half of it into the crater to share with the goddess. Kapiolani defiantly ate all the berries herself and then shouted down into the molten pit, "Jehovah is my God! I fear not Pele." Unscorched, she departed in triumph.

Among the islanders, generally, conditions were anything but what the missionaries had hoped for. Convicts, adventurers, thieves, and seamen turned harbor towns into centers of vice. The whaling seasons, when crews of lusty men landed and searched for women to help them celebrate on shore, were nightmares for the missionaries. The port town of Lahaina was described by a minister as "one of the breathing holes of hell."

The great American novelist Herman Melville, himself a whaler at one time, had much to say about

(15) With their slim, shallow boats and rounded oars, early Hawaiians were masters of the waters surrounding their islands.

(16) Any prince—and this early Hawaiian looks like one—would surely prize such a cloak and helmet made from tufts of bird feathers.

(17) There is no hint in this old engraving depicting a peaceful Hawaiian feast offering to Captain Cook of the violence that was to come.

COURTESY OF THE AMERICAN MUSEUM OF NATURAL HISTORY

(18) This "chef" holds what looks like a heavy potato masher. Actually, he is about to pound taro root into a paste, the basis of a Hawaiian food called poi.

COURTESY OF THE AMERICAN MUSEUM OF NATURAL HISTORY

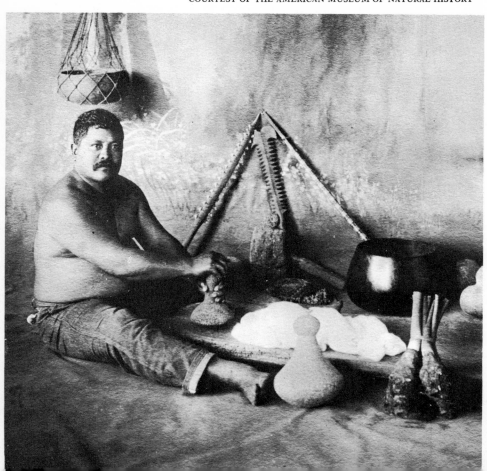

(19) These dignified hula dancers are as serious about their art as any classical ballerina.

(20) Surfing in Hawaii, the "sport of kings."

(21) When toy spears are wanted, boys such as these Western Australia Aborigines make their own.

(22) Bodily decorations are essential for important ceremonies among the Aborigines of north central Australia. Here, plant fibers are pasted on with clay and blood.

COURTESY OF THE AMERICAN
MUSEUM OF NATURAL HISTORY

(23) These First Australians are boldly curious in their inspection of an automobile—but one clings to a boomerang, just to be safe.

COURTESY OF THE AMERICAN
MUSEUM OF NATURAL HISTORY

(24) Ancient stories enacted in song
and dance are at the heart of the
tribal corroborees, as shown here
by native performers on stage.

AUSTRALIAN INFORMATION
SERVICE

(25) Patiently and artistically made,
these mosaic-like designs mark a
corroboree ground in central
Australia.

AUSTRALIAN INFORMATION
SERVICE

(26) While one hunter prepares to hurl a boomerang, his companion stands ready with his spear and spear thrower.

AUSTRALIAN INFORMATION
SERVICE

(27) There is no boredom expressed in the faces of these young pupils at an Australian settlement in the Northern Territory.

AUSTRALIAN INFORMATION
SERVICE

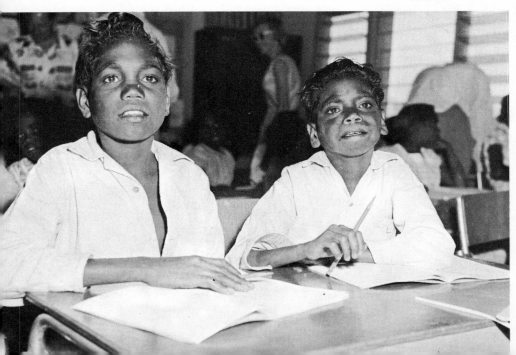

the debauchery that took place when seamen came ashore, and his book *Typee* is much concerned with the Hawaiians and primitives generally. He pitied the "poor savages" exposed to the "polluting examples" of the sailors. "Unsophisticated and confiding, they are easily led into every vice, and humanity weeps over the ruin thus remorselessly inflicted upon them by their European civilizers. Thrice happy are they who, inhabiting some yet undiscovered island in the midst of the ocean, have never been brought into contaminating contact with the white men."

The original band of missionaries, and those who followed, fought back against such excesses, preaching, exhorting, clothing the naked, campaigning against tobacco, destroying casks of rum, and generally impressing their own values on the population. Contributing to the missionaries' influence was their knowledge of reading, writing, and arithmetic, skills unknown to the islanders. The Hawaiians were apt pupils and eager to learn. Lacking books, they had relied on memory training to recite legends and lineage, and so could quickly repeat and recite what they were taught. They taught each other, making use of banana leaves or wet sand as tablets.

At the very beginning, the New Englanders had made a unique contribution to the islanders. For months, the hard-working preachers and their wives struggled to create a Hawaiian alphabet so that the natives could have books, especially the Bible, in their own language. They found some ninety-five different sounds in the language and realized that if they tried to create an alphabet of ninety-five characters, few persons could ever master it. By whittling and pruning, they reduced the new alphabet to a mere twelve letters. With them on their arrival, the missionaries had brought a secondhand press and type. Armed with this and their new alphabet, they proceeded to print the first pages ever to bear the Hawaiian language.

January 7, 1822, was a momentous day for them and for the Hawaiian people when, off the little press in Honolulu, came the sheets of what was to be an eight-page spelling book for the natives. Every chief there was invited to attend the event, and it was a solemn moment in Hawaii's history. Aside from the handful of boys who had been at school in Connecticut, no one in the whole Hawaiian kingdom could read or write. Within ten years there were nearly a thousand schools and a third of the population had some skill in reading and writing. It was the older natives who led the way. Classes were crowded with adults, even those with gray hair. Chiefs claimed priority and sat underlining the strange new words with their forefingers, sweating over their studies. Teachers swarmed to the schools. Native teachers developed. A call went out from all parts of the islands for books and more books.

Mass examinations of students' progress were held regularly. On these occasions, everybody flocked to the scene and the atmosphere was one of a celebration. This was especially so on the day when the schools from the entire Kona district were invited to participate in a mass examination at Kailua, Hawaii. The students, all adults, waited to begin their parade until after sunset. Then the crowds that had assembled to greet them were startled to see long lines of light illuminate the dark slope of the mountain sweeping up from the bay. From almost every direction came the marchers carrying torches. The lines finally merged into one broad, blazing column. The ranks then paused and thousands of conch shells were raised to the mouths of the marchers to produce a blast of sound. To Bingham the scene symbolized the arrival of the light of Christian teachings in the blackness of former paganism.

Year by year the missionaries worked at translating the New Testament into Hawaiian, printing each section as swiftly as it was finished. The islanders flocked to obtain copies, trading anything they had. The first complete edition of the New Testament was available in 1832, the Old Testament in 1839.

Along with this change to a new life way, there was a gradual decay of the population. When Cook arrived in 1778, he estimated that the islands' population might total around a half million. By 1823, a missionary census accounted for only 142,000; by the early 1850s that figure was reduced by half. Although Cook's estimate was probably exaggerated there was cause for alarm in the swiftly diminishing population. One of the islanders' own, David Malo, early educated by the missionaries, exclaimed in 1839, "The kingdom is sick. It is reduced to a skeleton, and is near to death; yea, the whole nation is near to a close."

One of the major reasons was the spreading of diseases brought in from the outside, especially syphilis which raged from one community to another. An epidemic that flared to its peak in 1805 is believed to have wiped out perhaps half of the inhabitants. But venereal disease remained the main, steady killer. Said David Malo, "Foreigners have lent their whole influence to make the Hawaiian Islands one great brothel." The result was that whole villages, including children, were affected. Family relationships were menaced by the lurking killer as well as by the changing social scene.

Perhaps the greatest threat to the stability of native social health was the "disease" of commerce. Both commoners and kings traded off whatever they had in order to supply themselves with liquor, tobacco, bright trinkets, and other goods usually far overpriced. So fond were Hawaiians of tobacco that pipe smoking was almost a universal habit, with even young children puffing at the imported weed. Alcoholism was also rampant. Kings and chiefs craved foreign luxuries they could not afford— yachts, horses and carriages, fancy uniforms, and expensive furniture, mortgaging themselves to tradesmen. High and low ended up in debt to merchants who usually had no concern about the people's welfare. The result was humiliation and dependence at the top, degradation and despair at the bottom.

At the peak of the whaling industry in 1846,

596 ships arrived in the islands. Most were American, with the British next in number. At first, Lahaina was the favored port but by 1850 the capital city of Honolulu was the commercial capital of the islands. It was a raw and roaring city packed with waterfront saloons, sheds, warehouses, New England church steeples, a Victorian-style royal palace, a complete conglomerate of styles and enterprises. Cattle for food on shipboard were driven down to the port through the streets. Forests were slashed for galley firewood. Pig sties, dried fish, slaughterhouses, all gave their special scents to the air. Lawlessness was the usual thing, and it was no help that shipmasters from Boston gave orders to discharge any troublesome crewmen in the islands. Native constables armed with canes could not cope with these castoffs nor with their pleasure-seeking shipmates.

There were other influences, exerted by American and British pioneers who saw agricultural and ranching potentials in the land. Ranching became a big-scale industry, though the hungry herds of cattle chomped the hillsides into bareness. After the introduction of the horse, in 1803, horses were everywhere by 1860. Hawaiians, male and female, took to riding these as skillfully as they had ridden their surfboards. And all the while, *haoles* carried on their experiments with various agricultural products—cotton and coffee, grapes and wheat. For a time there was a big trade in coffee production, then in Irish potatoes. Both crops failed to live up to their planters' hopes. Other money-making schemes included raising silkworms or importing trees to reforest the denuded mountains.

What was to become the main product had been quietly growing in the background, the wild sugar cane that flourished without attention. The natives chewed it raw for its sweetness, or used clumps of it for windbreaks, and cut its leaves to thatch huts. While certain foreign experimenters tried growing imported varieties of plants, more conservative growers concentrated on sugar cane. A few, small pioneer mills ground the cane into sugar, but there was no extensive sugar planting until about 1835 when an American firm leased land on Kauai. Managers of the plantation established there struggled on for years without any marked success. But interest in developing better plants and mills continued so the export of sugar became a growing business. Around 1870 the sugar trade was the main source of prosperity in the islands and in 1875 a treaty was signed between Hawaii and the United States so that sugar and other specified articles of trade could enter the States without duty. This led to a strengthening of American influence in the islands and to a boom in sugar production. Much capital was invested in the sugar industry by Americans, particularly by Claus Spreckels who had already made a fortune as a sugar refiner in California.

Spreckels and the sugar industry are synonymous today, like James Dole and pineapples. On the outskirts of Honolulu, Dole built a pineapple canning factory that was to become the world's largest of its kind.

Whether raising sugar cane or pineapples, the big need of the owners was for laborers in the fields. The native Hawaiian stock was dying off, and those who survived had little interest in laboring with a hoe and machete. Working for wages was a far different thing from the old days when work had been simply a part of life, essential but also an occasion for community cooperation and harvest feasts.

So, the search for strong backs and stout hands to mine the wealth of the plantations led to a series of invasions from foreign lands in the form of imported labor. Missionaries, without considering Hawaiian traditions or desires, had envisioned a land in which small, family-sized farms would dot the islands. But though there was a general reparceling of land, most of the islanders did not take advantage of their opportunity to claim sites for themselves. They did not understand why individual farms were desirable and were more involved in exploring their increased freedom under the declining power of the kings, which permitted them to rove about according to whim. Instead of land, they coveted the clothes and gadgets of the *haoles,* and tended to flock to the cities. In the place of many small farms, big plantations fattened and expanded, with nobody reliable to work them.

Chinese had been employed at various times in the sugar mills and had proved to be reliable and industrious. So, the plantation owners looked toward China for more recruits. A ship was dispatched to Hong Kong, its captain ordered to scout for the hard-working coolies. In January 1852, the ship returned with nearly two hundred. Six months later another one hundred arrived, the first of tens of thousands to come. So many Chinese came that the dominant white interests became worried about being overwhelmed, especially as thousands of the Chinese settled down to stay when they had completed their five-year labor agreements. They became shopkeepers and businessmen on their own. The term "yellow peril" was as frightening to many whites as the scare-term "red communism" was to be some hundred years later in the then forty-eight United States.

In 1868, the Hawaiian government under Kamehameha V, stationed a consulate in Japan. Around one hundred and fifty Japanese were persuaded to sign three-year contracts as laborers on the plantations. This experiment was not immediately successful and other immigrants were brought in: Portuguese, German, Norwegian, and Madeirans off the African coast of Morocco. When these did not work out as well as hoped, plantation managers turned toward Japan again. As a result of a withering drought and consequent famine in Japan, starving peasants were eager to emigrate to another locale. They appeared in hordes before the recruiting agents, beginning in 1886. Two thousand shipped out the first year. Others followed until nearly two hundred thousand had landed in Honolulu, and though most did not intend to stay, a great many did and became

absorbed into the increasingly mixed population. Fili-
pinos, too, joined the melting pot.

Around the 1870s, tourism became a source of
prosperity to the islands. Inns and hotels sprang up to
accommodate visitors. Towns became modernized, although many natives—their numbers steadily declining—
lived in thatched houses as they had done for centuries.
Still, the impact of Western ways showed in their habits
and ways of dress. The loose Mother Hubbards of the
women were abandoned for confining dresses and uncom-
fortable corsets. Men who had never known shoes still
often went barefoot on country roads, but carried squeaky,
stiff leather shoes of modern make to put on when they
arrived at the city.

Disease among the natives was still rife. Smallpox killed huge numbers. Leprosy, one of the most
dreaded diseases, came into the realm during the rule of
Kamehameha III, possibly from China. It spread over
the islands until the government decided that the only
treatment possible was to isolate the victims on a barren
peninsula on the north side of the island of Molokai.
By 1873, about eight hundred patients, mostly natives,
were settled in this leper station. Even though family
ties had been badly raveled as old traditions vanished,
enough family feeling remained to make parents and
relatives feel desperate at the thought of having members
of their group taken away, certain they were being taken
to be killed. As the authorities sought out the lepers,
natives hid diseased relatives and friends in caves, under

brush, and in forests. From these hiding places the sufferers sought out whatever native priests remained, or consulted miracle-promising quacks.

The islanders had always considered that they were special interests of Beritani—as they pronounced Britain—and for a time it seemed that Great Britain would annex the islands. However, it was the United States that became the more solidly entrenched, having the greater economic and strategic interests. Some islanders resisted outside influence and there was a very strong movement in favor of Hawaii for the Hawaiians, beginning in the 1840s. In spite of all the alien influences there was a clinging to old ways and beliefs. Ancient *kapu* sites were still honored by many, natives placing furtive offerings there as their ancestors had done. Still, because of the stern disapproval of the missionaries, only a few dared to engage in the once universal sport of surfing. The art had almost disappeared by the end of the century.

The Hawaiian kings, also, were losing their powers, being mainly figureheads ruled by outside interests, especially those of the United States. Among the last to put up resistance was Kalakaua. When he died during a journey to San Francisco in 1891, his sister Liliuokalani, the last of the native Hawaiian rulers, became queen. She was determined, like her brother, to restore the authority of the crown. She failed in the face of machinations by opposing powers. Also, the outbreak of the Spanish-American War led to an influx of American soldiers to island ports, among them Pearl Harbor. That harbor had been leased to the United States in 1887. There was increased American pressure for annexation of the islands because of their military value during such far-flung wars as the Spanish-American conflict. In the summer of 1898 the Congress passed a resolution to annex Hawaii, and so, after due ceremonies, it became a territory of the United States. The embittered and articulate Liliuokalani protested, but it was no use. The long road of the Hawaiian monarchy was at an end. The paths made centuries before were lost among the thriving plantations and hotels. Ancient customs were distorted and commercialized. The natives themselves were facing extinction.

A good many persons, including Americans, had never heard of Pearl Harbor before the Japanese air force devastated the United States' naval and air installations there on December 7, 1941, an act which plunged the two nations into bitter warfare. Among the most distinguished Hawaiians who fought back against the armies of the Japanese Emperor were the descendants of the early Japanese who had come to Hawaii. A final count of Hawaiian war casualties showed that 80 per cent of those killed and 88 per cent of those wounded were of Japanese ancestry. One of the arguments of mainlanders opposed to statehood for Hawaii had been that the high percentage of Japanese, the largest ethnic group at the time of the Second World War, was that the loyalty of the Japanese was questionable and that they presented the old "yellow peril" threat. The valiant record of these Nisei, or Japanese Americans, reduced such arguments to hollow murmurings. In 1959, Hawaii was admitted to the Union.

Hawaii as it had once been was barely a memory at the end of the war. Ever since 1840, school attendance had been compulsory for all islanders under the age of fourteen. From 1850 on, teaching in English gradually replaced that in Hawaiian. Hawaiians and part Hawaiians made up a large majority of the public school students until the 1890s when Chinese, Portuguese, and Japanese children enrolled in growing numbers. Children of the whites mostly attended private schools, so in spite of the general integration at one level, there was segregation of a kind. Within the mixed groups at public schools, there was a "pecking order," certain racial groups having a higher status than others. The influx of soldiers and the interchange of social patterns during World War II helped to shake up this kind of structure and stimulate increased opportunities of education for everyone, regardless of ancestry. Vocational schools, the widespread state library system, the increasing numbers of scholars and teachers attracted to the University of Hawaii, and investment by private companies in commercial production, all added up to an economically thriving new American state.

Tourism after the war became a lucrative source of income in the islands. Droves of visitors arrived, lured by advertising that featured the islands as the nation's showcase of racial harmony, together with its temperate climate and relaxed living. Surfboarding was revived not only by the Hawaiians but by enthusiastic visitors. Today, this "sport of kings" is one of the few remaining links with the aboriginal past.

The real kings and queens are gone. The elaborate hula dances are reduced to parodies in which visiting *haoles* awkwardly join in to the rhythm of non-native guitars and ukuleles. High-rise hotels loom against the skyline at Waikiki. The hammer of pile drivers, the snarl of caterpillars and cement trucks is so loud the mayor of Honolulu created a Committee on Noise. At night, teen-agers cruise the streets, filling the once trade-wind-swept air with gasoline fumes. The making of leis is a solid business with a trade association to control prices. "Beach boys" are hired to teach guests to surf ride as part of a commercial routine.

Hired islanders in canoes still paddle out to meet the huge ocean liners coming in with their loads of tourists, imitating the old days when villagers went out spontaneously to welcome visiting ships. Very few full-blood Hawaiians remain, and even fewer recall either the community work or community celebrations of the long ago. The aboriginal arts—the feathered cloaks, carved images, hand-hewn bowls and canoes—are labeled and displayed in museums. What is left of the former culture is mainly in the hands of collectors and scholars. The native Hawaiian has become one more member of the great melting pot that has mixed so many races into what is called American. In effect, the original Hawaiians have vanished, making up a small minority of the population. With them went certain admirable values, as well as some less admirable in modern eyes. What Hawaii becomes in the future will be largely what the United States as a whole becomes.

4.
Sand,
Sun, and
Water Holes

AUSTRALIAN ABORIGINES

The little tent standing in the sun-seared landscape was the only sign of human habitation. Extending from it in all directions was the blue-gray and ocher-red scrubland, its clumps of spinifex grass swaying in the desert winds. Mottled lizards flicked through the grass roots, and at a nearby water hole a solitary kangaroo drank. A stand of acacia trees provided shade for the woman who came out of the tent and scanned the landscape.

She was a slender woman, graying hair visible under her sailor hat, her face lightly shadowed by the fly veil hanging from its brim. In spite of her crude camping equipment—kerosene tins for hauling water, a brushwood shelter for supplies, and a prickle bush fence that enclosed a kind of yard—she wore a white blouse, stiff collar and ribbon tie, a long dark skirt, and gloves. The woman's name was Daisy Bates and she had left her homeland in England while Victoria was still queen. Though the queen had died in 1901, some twenty years before, Mrs. Bates clung to Victorian dress. Nor did she ever emerge from her solitary tent, wherever it might be pitched in the Australian bush, without being carefully clothed and groomed. Now, as she searched the landscape, she saw far off a single line of human beings marching toward her. Obviously, they had seen the smoke from her campfire and were on their way to "sit down" with her as others of their kind had done during the many years she had made her camps in the land of the Aborigines. As the small band approached, she saw that they, like the other "black fellows" she had known, were either naked or half clothed in rags. The man, carrying a wooden spear, led, while his wives and children plodded in the rear. Daisy Bates poked the still-warm ashes of last night's fire, put on more fuel, and prepared to make tea and damper cakes for her Stone Age guests.

A widow, who had inherited a cattle ranch in Australia, Mrs. Bates had become keenly interested in the Aborigines during a visit to Australia in 1889. She had been a journalist, and had a gift for languages. Having read that the Aborigines were being treated cruelly by the settlers of Western Australia, she investigated. Though she found no evidences of deliberate cruelty, she did find that there was extensive misery among the Aborigines and that their ranks were swiftly diminishing. Using her private resources, she went out to live among them, helping them, studying them, and making such a place for herself in their lives that they traveled hundreds of miles to see her, calling her *Kabbarli,* Grandmother. In turn, she called these non-literate people—some of them cannibals who ate their own children—"my children."

No one knows exactly where these early Australians came from although it is generally thought that they migrated from Asia between ten thousand or twenty thousand years ago. The English who established their first permanent settlement in Sydney, Australia, in 1788 referred to the natives as black men, but their skin color varies and most are a chocolate brown. Their hair is curly or wavy, ranging from brown to black, and the children often have blond or red hair that darkens as they mature.

At the time that the English decided to use Australia as a dumping ground for the convicts over-crowding their prisons in 1788, there were an estimated three hundred thousand Aborigines on the continent that is about five times the size of Alaska. Aside from a few brief visits by early day ships they were isolated from the outside world. With the most rudimentary tools and no knowledge of agriculture, they managed to survive in even the most barren areas such as the desert interior. If they happened to live near the sea or rivers they had fish to eat. Otherwise, they existed mostly on small game, insects, and wild plants. Game, in arid lands, sometimes consisted of nothing more than snakes, lizards, desert rats, and locusts, and even these could require that the hunters search over twenty or more miles a day, traveling by way of the precious water holes or sinks. The men with their wooden spears or boomerangs hunted for larger game while the women scoured the earth for ants, grubs, roots, and seeds. Sometimes it could take two hours of patient search and labor for a woman to gather as much as a handful of seeds which she mashed into a rough flour. With a digging stick she unearthed yams and edible roots. The Aborigines did no planting.

They knew how to make fire, in which they baked their lizards or, when lucky, a kangaroo. Those who lived on the coast found food more easily than those in the arid, central regions of the continent. All were a hardy people, living constantly outdoors in boiling noons and frigid nights. They built no permanent houses or villages; at the most, they might erect a crude shelter of branches called a wurley or lean-tos of bark. They seldom wore clothing. In cold regions they made use of the skins of kangaroos and opossums but these were not fashioned into garments; they were simply thrown over the shoulders or used as a blanket. Males wore waist belts woven from human hair, for decoration and for a support from which to dangle small game. When of an age to marry, girls wore a belt or fringe of bark. Bark was used, too, for containers, and kangaroo hide for bags.

The Aborigine, being primarily a hunter and

food gatherer, had no need of permanent housing. Survival demanded that he keep roving in search of sustenance, and he could not afford to carry anything extra in the way of possessions. Only the most essential articles were carried by a family or band—spears and spear throwers, digging sticks, fire sticks, bark bags and baskets, stone axes, and sacred objects made of wood, stone, and quartz. In fishing regions, bone hooks and lines and nets made from vegetable fiber would be part of the baggage.

The boomerang was often included although not all tribes possessed it. Essentially, a boomerang is a throwing stick especially shaped to sail through the air and strike its victim with force. There were different kinds of boomerangs, some for hunting, some for fighting, some used as musical instruments for tapping out rhythms, and the "returning" boomerang which would circle back to the thrower's hand. The latter was most often used to bring down birds, especially along the coast.

Earliest visitors to Australia considered these people "utter barbarians," and an English voyager in 1688 described them as "the miserablist people in the whole world." They did not regard themselves as miserable and they had one special quality that set them apart from most primitive peoples (and modern, as well) in that they appear to have been among the most unwarlike folk known in history. None seem to have carried on organized warfare as we know it. However, if during a gathering of clans for trade bad feeling developed between individuals, a formal confrontation might take place, somewhat like a duel. An offended man and his offender would hurl insults and spears at each other, but even this was a kind of mock combat and was brought to a halt when, in the judgment of the group at large, "honor" had been upheld, or when there was danger of serious injury.

When the earliest of the Aborigines straggled across the continent they gradually settled into separate bands, each with its own sacred totems, chants, moral codes, and religion. Before the coming of the Europeans it is estimated that there were about five hundred groups of various sizes, each group speaking the same language or dialect, having similar local customs, and living within a definite territory. If the area of ownership was on the fertile coastal fringe where food was relatively plentiful, the tribal territory might be no more than fifty square miles. In the desert region, the Arunta tribe occupied over twenty-five thousand square miles. Whatever the size of the tribal claim, the members never sat still within its boundaries. Even if there was plentiful food and water they would settle down for no more than a few weeks or months before wandering again. In the arid plains they moved constantly, searching for food and water or visiting sacred sites. But each band respected the boundaries of another. A group's particular territory was sacred to its members, being their physical and spiritual home.

Each clan, or moiety, was regarded as descended from a plant or animal. One clan's totem might be a kangaroo, another's an emu—a totem being considered as related by blood to a given family or clan and taken as its symbol. A member of the kangaroo clan respected the living animal as if it were a relative, and though he might eat it, he was careful to avoid certain forbidden parts of its flesh—usually parts that were not highly desired. Wherever an Aborigine might roam, he always considered that his true home was where his totem dwelled. So, regularly, he would perform a "walkabout" to his home territory, a semireligious rite in which he sought to contact the local spirits and renew ties with them. Stones could be sacred—some were believed to have the power of impregnating women who walked by them. Boards ornamented with symbols of spirit beings and certain hallowed objects such as trees or hollow logs were considered sacred. Some ornamented boards bore the figures of game animals—snakes, birds, kangaroos, crocodiles. The men in their ceremonies imitated the movements of the animals in dances as formal as ballet.

Ceremonies, magic, and sorcery played a vital role in Aboriginal culture, expressing the hopes and fears of the people. Sacred myths were retold and enacted. The myths were complex, the whole religion highly mystic. What we think of as creation the Aborigines conceived of as the "dream time," a concept made more difficult by the fact that to them dreams were as much a part of reality as wakefulness. Everything, in a sense, existed in the dream time, the world of the present and the eternal being coexistent.

The clan was not a political unit and there were no tribal chiefs. There were instead elders, "clever men," who were full of experience and had a thorough knowledge of mythology and ritual. Social relationships were governed by very strict laws and taboos, and family relationships extended far beyond the immediate family group. One's father, for instance, and his brothers were all called "father" by the Aborigines. The same was true of a mother and her sisters. The kinship system regulated the social life, including marriage. A man could marry only a woman who was in the approved kinship category within his group, and only relatives could speak to each other. The roles for males and females were carefully separated, the religious symbols and rites being the realm of the males. Certain religious symbols such as ritual boards painted with yellow, red, and black patterns were not to be seen by women's eyes. Nor could women observe or have anything to do with the secret rituals which introduced a boy into manhood. If she did, she had to be put to death at once. In the same way, men were excluded from the rituals surrounding girls at puberty. The sacred dancing was done by the men, but women could join in the secular dances. There were a limited number of musical instruments, the chief one being the *didjeridoo,* a wind instrument made from the branch of the trunk of a tree hollowed out by white ants. When blown it made a deep, booming sound. The most enjoyed social event was the corroboree, a series of ceremonial dances that could continue night after night for about two weeks. Successful hunts were celebrated by a corroboree. For this, the men would ornament their bodies with strips of red ocher and white pipe clay, head crests of feathers, and their belts and tassels reddened with their own blood, taken from deliberate cuts in their flesh. Sometimes they would trace designs of blood on their chests and then paste on these down from the breasts of birds.

When the earliest shipload of convicts and their guards arrived in Australia, Captain Arthur Phillip had his first glimpse of the Aborigines around Botany Bay. Captain Phillip tried to encourage friendship by holding out beads and red cloth, telling the marines with him to lay down their muskets. The Aborigines dropped their spears and clubs and the two groups came cautiously together. When the white men began erecting their tents, the natives withdrew and watched from a distance.

In time, some of the Aborigines let themselves be coaxed into the new settlement and willingly helped the whites in small ways. The brief harmony was doomed. Even though the Aboriginal women were not attractive by European standards, the white men soon sought them out, against orders, and abducted them. Sometimes they dragged forth girls only ten years old and bashed in the heads of their male protectors with the butts of their guns. Convicts, wandering off from their enforced labor projects, helped themselves to the canoes, spears, or other articles the Aborigines left unguarded.

As more shiploads of unruly convicts and their keepers arrived, the Aborigines' resentment deepened. Already they had been infected by the strangers' diseases. Smallpox was especially fatal. From 1789 on, the Europeans began to stumble onto the pockmarked bodies lying dead in the bush or on the beaches. Before long, one half of the native population of Sydney was wiped out. In time, smallpox would destroy one third or more of the Aboriginal population. Bullets, too, cut down the Aborigines as the whites advanced farther into their territories.

Most Europeans considered that the natives could never be civilized, and that they were a worthless people with no culture. At a public meeting in Sydney in 1826, leaders of the community declared that the Aborigine was not a human being and that there was no more wrong in shooting him than a dingo, a native wild dog. Shooting was not the main threat to the Aborigine. The taking over of huge tracts of his land for farming or grazing was worse, for with the land went his whole way of life. Unable to live off the land, he became dependent on charity and on rations distributed by the government.

Once the Aborigine had been a nomadic hunter, wandering freely. With no more room to wander, cut off from his spiritual homelands, the Aborigine began to settle down in permanent camps on the fringes of the white settlements. Men, women, and children took to roaming the towns, begging for handouts. Work for wages was completely outside the Aboriginal's tradition. Nor had he ever been interested in acquiring personal possessions.

(28) Small huts, small people. Pygmies appearing at an American exposition in St. Louis.

(29) Lighting the long pipe is a serious affair for the two young men, but the rest of the Pygmy family have their own interests.

(30) It takes muscular bodies likes these of the Kalahari Bushmen to survive in a harsh environment.

(31)

The old one, the maiden, the young mother and child—each a part of the Kalahari scene.

(32)

A new generation of Peri Village, Manus, New Guinea, greets anthropologist Dr. Margaret Mead.

(33) Here comes the bride (standing on a carved wooden bed on the platform of a canoe). Admiralty Islands.

(34) No water wings or rubber floats are needed by these water-dwelling Manus children.

(35)

Not a flat stone face with two holes for eyes, but a highly prized Yap "money" disk, a symbol of wealth.

(36) The spears and blowguns of Jivaro warriors are no match for modern machines taking over these South American Indians' land.

(37) Milking a reindeer is no problem,
if you are a Lapp.

(38) Lapp porters can make a land
traveler's journey easier—and
those long staves may come in
handy, too.

(39) Old ways—the robes, sashes, and tattooed lips of the women—remain in this group of Ainus from Japan.

Propertyless, disinherited, he became a miserable outcast, living on scraps like a stray animal. With the mixing of European and Aboriginal blood, the Aborigine could no longer trace his vital kinship lines. The ancient rules governing marriage broke down, and the authority of the old men weakened as some of the younger men began to work for the settlers and took over what leadership there was by virtue of their providing extra rations earned from their employers.

By 1900, the Aborigines' situation was desperate. In Perth, Daisy Bates found only two surviving Aborigines of the original large group that had ruled over many hundreds of square miles of the area seventy years before. These were an old man and an old woman. The old man survived longer but with his death in 1907 came the end of the Perth tribe. Many other tribes had met extinction, their hunting grounds buried under buildings and streets, their bee trees cut down to make way for sheep, cattle, crops, and telegraph lines. Younger generations openly flouted old laws. Some became thieves. Half-castes, whom the Aborigines despised, increased.

Not all white settlers were unkind or thoughtless, and British officials back in the mother country wrote laws prescribing humane treatment of the Aborigines but in the "outback" of the huge Australian continent, killings, massacres, and even poisonings took place. England sent missionaries to educate and convert the natives, but it was almost impossible for the Aborigines to grasp what

Christianity was all about, or to understand the strange workings of the white man's society.

One of the first acts of the missionaries was to force clothes onto the natives. Knowing nothing of soap and water, the usual result was that trousers and shirts, or dresses, became stiff with dirt and provided extra hiding places for germs or lice. One earnest missionary built twenty-eight tidy houses for his dark-skinned flock and allotted a piece of land to each family. The families felt suffocated in their walled "prisons," shut off from the worlds of wind, sun, and stars. They pined, sickened, and died. To outside natives watching the corpse of a kinsman being removed from a house, the house seemed obviously a place of death. Those who were persuaded to take up residence in the same place were so convinced that it was a death sentence, they commonly perished in turn.

After the death of the last Perth native, Daisy Bates set out on a two-year pilgrimage through the Southwest, through all the old tribal grounds that had become railway cities and towns. She sought the living remnants of the various clans—those of the turkey totem, opossum, and mallee hen. Many were extinct. Wherever she went, she made notes, and learned to speak the natives' language. Above all, she tried to comfort and sustain the wretched people. In her book *The Passing of the Aborigines* she wrote that she became the natives' ancestral grandmother and that she lived their lives, not her own. She established her first tent home in 1914 on hills west of Fowler's Bay. There she had three blind and helpless natives on her hands. Daily, she hunted rabbits and lizards for them, cooked their meals, lighted their pipes, and sometimes led them by means of a long pole for walks in their beloved bush. It was she who had to bury them when they died.

During the construction of the Australian transcontinental railroad, Daisy Bates climaxed her long service to a dispossessed race. In the fall of 1919, she went to a railroad siding called the Ooldea Soak, an unfailing source of water in barren central Australia. There she pitched her little tent. The construction of the railroad had meant the despoilment of native groups all along the way. As trains began to pass over the lines, white people would toss trinkets or bits of food to Aborigines watching from the embankments. Construction crews gave some their first taste of alcohol. The news of such gifts spread throughout the region and before long, natives began marching toward the railroad, sometimes from distances over a thousand miles away. They believed that eventually the railroad and the whites connected with it would disappear, leaving tools and various goods for them.

When Mrs. Bates arrived, hundreds of derelict natives had set up their wurley at the sidings, living on scraps tourists tossed to them from the train. Prostitution was usual among the Aboriginal women who mingled with railroad workers. When the first half-caste babies were born, the frantic mothers thought the lighter skin color meant the infants were sick, perhaps as the result of the mothers eating white men's food. There was uncertainty among the Aborigines as to exactly how babies were conceived, due to the "impregnating stones" and the need for fathers to "dream" the infants into being. The mothers rubbed the infants frantically with charcoal to restore their dark color, and in the process the babies sometimes died.

Naked or clothed in castoff rags, often ravaged by disease, they turned to the white woman among them for help. When an epidemic of influenza broke out, Mrs. Bates labored every hour of the day, and miraculously stretched what food and tea she had to share with them. During the summer of her first year at Ooldea, 120-degree weather was common, and there were blinding dust storms. She was asked by the government to arrange for a display of the Aborigines in honor of His Royal Highness, the Prince of Wales, who was to pass through Ooldea on a tour of Australia. Not all the Aborigines had forgotten their former independence, and some muttered angrily at the white man's usurping their lands, shooting kangaroos and leaving their bodies to rot, or monopolizing precious water holes for the hated camels that caravans employed in desert travel. So, on an April day in 1920, before the Prince's arrival, an angry mob of eighty men came blustering toward the little tent.

"Black fella king belong to this country!" one of the leaders shouted. "We don't want *waijela* (white fella) here!" Another exclaimed, "This is our country. You send paper to the Gubamint, tell 'em we don't want white fella king."

Even for Daisy Bates it was a touchy situation, with only fifteen white settlers nearby and the closest policeman 170 miles away. She made tea and told the natives that the white king would bring them many gifts, including pipes and flour. Also, she told them that if they had a native black king, they would also have to have a native black queen. Though they had little concept of any ruler, the very notion of having a native woman ruler was abhorrent to them. So they gave in and when the Prince of Wales did pass through, they and others joined in a hearty welcome, decked out in corroboree paint and feathers.

Later, Mrs. Bates moved her tent to a sandy gully a mile north of the tracks, feeling that the proximity of the trains helped to undo her work with the natives. At her new location, on a trail to the Soak, she remained for sixteen years. Natives came to her from all directions, sometimes spending two years on the journey, zigzagging through the desert in search of food and water, following the tracks of those who had gone ahead. Each time a new group appeared, the groups already established near the tent would announce the new arrivals by wailing, shouting, and rattling spears. Always their "grandmother" welcomed the strangers with "tucker" (food) and tea. As soon as the newcomers had satisfied their curiosity over the distant trains, the houses of the white settlers, and the taste of sugar and tea, they became bold enough to go to the sidings, for the biscuits and fruit thrown to them. Sometimes they exchanged their boomerangs or spears for a shilling or sixpence, promptly spending the money on whatever caught their fancy. Mrs. Bates wrote that of all the hundreds who "sat down" with her there, not one ever returned to his natural bush life.

But they did have to hunt in the vicinity to add to their rations. The kangaroo and emu had become rare; rabbits introduced by white men had taken their place. The greatest loss to the "black fellows," however, and to Daisy Bates was that pipelines and pumping plants at the Soak destroyed the water source so that by the fall of 1926 the Soak was dry. White-haired now, the English woman began carrying water from another source a mile away, going back and forth at least twice a day, in scorching temperatures.

The water was for drinking and cooking, and her own uses in cleanliness. She never forced the natives to the ordeal of soap and water but encouraged them to use clean olive oil to remove the worst of their dirt and odors. Also, she used native medicines such as soft white ash in treating wounds.

Before she ended her long service at Ooldea she was honored by being made a Commander of the Order of the British Empire. Daisy Bates had planned to finish out her life among the natives but she decided that she must save the many notes she had made on their culture and give the world the story of their plight. In 1936, at the age of seventy-four, she left Ooldea. On the day she started off to await the train, the natives followed, crooning and crying. Because she had some of the sacred totem boards in her possession, the women dared not come close, still governed by ancient taboos. Seven boxes of manuscripts went with Mrs. Bates, to become part of the world's knowledge of the Australian Aborigine. At Adelaide, Daisy Bates lived out the ninety years of her existence.

In recognizing the value of her work among the Aborigines, the government helped to show that it was not indifferent to the well-being of these people. At first it seemed that the Aborigines would solve the problem by simply "dying out," as another indigenous people, the Tasmanians, had done. Actually, the Tasmanians had been literally hunted to death, the British Parliament having decreed that they were non-human and could be shot like game. Although the large, British-owned island of Tasmania is separated only by Bass Strait from Melbourne, Australia, the natives there were of a different stock from the mainland Aborigines, being Negroid. (A special term "Australoid" was invented for the continental Aborigines.) The Tasmanians' first contact with white men was in 1772 when a French explorer landed on their shores. Later came the English. Within seventy-three years, the last of what has been estimated as anywhere from two thousand to seven thousand Tasmanians died.

With the belief that the Aborigines, too, would perish, together with the conviction that they were too inferior ever to adapt to Australian society, the British government considered them to be wards of the state. Though they were to be regarded as British subjects, they were to live apart from the Europeans. In order to achieve their isolation, reserves were established and the government assumed responsibility for not letting the natives starve. Beyond that, little was done. In 1825, a change came in the general attitude of the Crown toward native peoples in its widespread empire. They were to be civilized and converted to Christianity.

Australian officialdom ignored the new policy and continued to segregate the Aborigines as before, the majority still insisting that they could not be civilized. It was easy enough to justify this attitude by pointing out the squalor of the natives' life, whether on camps at the fringes of settlements or on the reserves. Employers who tried to use them as workers found that they had no conception of time and, if paid in money instead of rations, would promptly squander their earnings. Or, at any moment, they might leave their jobs simply out of restlessness for a "walkabout," or a desire to visit a shrine where the spirits of their ancestors were.

By the 1930s, however, there was a growing uneasiness about the isolation, wardship policy. The Aborigines were not dying out; therefore some more positive approach was needed. A new policy was designed at the capital city Canberra, in 1937. The authorities in conference there decreed that mixed-blood Aborigines should be assimilated into modern Australian society. Not much later, the same policy was adopted in regard to full bloods.

Decreeing that the Aborigines were to become a part of the society was easier decided than done. In spite of the majority's dependence on handouts from government or church, and the general breakdown of their culture, centuries of mythology and social custom were not easily abandoned. They still had not developed any deep yearning for white men's goods except as toys or objects of curiosity, generally preferring their crude digging sticks and spears. As for the white man's warfare, nothing in their background gave them an understanding of it. They were familiar with killing as a form of retribution against an individual who had broken a tribal law, but they could not conceive of why whites would go out with armies to kill people they did not even know. Uprooted, in limbo, the Aborigines lived from day to day, hour to hour, caring for little beyond survival and not greatly interested even in that.

The governmental assimilation program proceeded slowly; Christian missions, financed by their own memberships, could barely survive. Then came the disruption of the Second World War in which the survival of the British Empire itself was at stake. The fate of the Aborigines was easily forgotten even though the military impinged on almost every portion of the continent, including remote areas where some tribes still clung to their nomadic, primitive life. Large military camps grew up quickly in formerly unexplored regions. By the war's end, there were very few natives who had not been exposed to white contact.

Preceding 1954, government settlements for the natives were mainly simple depots where agents distributed rations and tobacco when the tribes wandered in from the outside. Some wanderers stayed, having nowhere else to go, settling down in their flimsy wurley. But once the assimilation program got into full stride, government money came pouring in. New schools, hospitals, houses, and dispensaries were built. Whereas in 1954 the director of welfare had less than $100,000 to spend and a staff of under sixty, in 1966 he had over $4 million and a staff of over five hundred to promote Aboriginal health, hygiene, education, and training for employment. For every seventy Aborigines there was one government officer or missionary working full time in the field.

Up until a referendum in May 1967, leading to changes in the Australian constitution, Aborigines were not included in the census count. As of 1970, the Aboriginal population stood at about forty-five thousand full bloods and seventy-seven thousand half bloods. The number of Aborigines, including full bloods, is increasing more than the Australian average. Though scattered over the entire continent, the majority of natives are in Western Australia, Queensland, and the Northern Territory. In New South Wales and Victoria, most are of mixed blood. The federal government has created an Office of Aboriginal Affairs and its stated policy is to preserve and encourage Aboriginal pride in past culture at the same time that it seeks to help the Aborigines to become an integral part of Australian community life.

One of the chief factors working against successful assimilation of the natives was, and is, racial prejudice. In some places today Aborigines and whites share common living areas, but there is little intermingling. In some regions it is not uncommon for whites to try to prevent the Aborigines from moving into their towns. Nor are the Aborigines united in a search for a new status. Old ties with local groups carry over and attempt at organizations for a common goal fail because of ancient animosities. Fear of sorcery from certain traditional enemies lingers on, and even mixed bloods in metropolitan Sydney claim that mixed bloods from parts of New South Wales are "bad mobs." The road to full assimilation is bound to be a long one. Most adult Aborigines lack education or the motivation to enter into white society even if they are welcomed. The fact that it is now considered proper to call them the First Australians instead of blacks or Aborigines does not basically change their situation. Laws giving the First Australian the right to vote or to buy liquor does not at the same time mean that he can quickly shift from being a hunter of frogs or lizards to being a bank clerk or mechanic.

The main hope for absorbing the Aborigines into the modern world lies in the education of the young, and compulsory education is now a law. A majority of youngsters are handicapped at home by bad housing and by their parents' ignorance or indifference to learning. Yet, some manage to pass through high school to become nurses, clerical workers, and teachers.

Some of the younger Aboriginal males are finding more opportunities for employment. The mixed bloods are favored and usually they are employed at manual chores requiring no special skills. In the Northwest, however, on the large cattle ranches most of the stockmen are half-blood Aborigines. They are agile, rugged horsemen and have adopted Western cowboy attire—heeled boots, tight jeans, slouch hats. At a typical ranch, the Aboriginal cowboys and their relatives live in a separate compound, coming and going at will so that the ranch manager is never certain just how many are there. The manager gives out free food rations once a week, and a cake of soap and a packet of chewing tobacco are included. Free clothes are distributed several times a year. Money means little to most, although the old people who draw a full Commonwealth pension have a certain status among the "modernized" natives. If women want to work there are opportunities in the vegetable garden, the house, the laundry.

But all this, though it provides such groups with food and shelter, does not restore their pride or give real meaning to their lives.

There are perhaps around six thousand Aborigines in the desert regions of northern and western Australia who still pursue at least a semitraditional tribal life. Isolated though they are, they are visited by government patrol officers, missionaries, and scientific expeditions. And, periodically, they go to mission and government stations for medical aid or for food and water when their own supplies run out.

In the necessarily slow process of assimilation

(certain Australians think the government is pushing it too fast) much will be lost. The communal way of life, in which each shared with the group whatever essentials he had, will go. Even today this tradition is so strong that Aboriginal children have to be encouraged to be aggressive like the majority of their white playmates. An Aborigine who may have a skill that makes him employable in a city finds that when he returns to his home grounds for a vacation, everything he may have bought for himself— new clothes, a radio, a cigarette lighter—must be shared with all his relatives, no matter how distant. Communal sharing, once a virtue and a necessity, becomes an obstacle to the individual's incentive to accumulate more money and more goods as Western mores demand.

The Aboriginals of Arnhem Land believed the Milky Way was a vast river of water lily bulbs, food for the star people. The Southern Cross they saw as a band of hunters who caught a snake; they had eaten it and their eyes became so brilliant they could be seen from the earth. The shape of Orion suggested a boatload of fishermen. Every day the feminine sun walked across the sky with her digging sticks; after slipping below the horizon she turned herself into a wallaby, a small kangaroo, and hopped back to her starting point.

Now that the "man in the moon" has become actual men on the moon, the Aborigines, like all other human beings, are bound to perceive that what was once a source of poetry and mythology is in fact an apparently lifeless sphere littered with dreary rocks. No doubt new legends will replace the old, but for Aboriginal and modern man alike they will be legends of jet planes, lunar landers, and space flight.

Here and there, some groups of Aborigines are aware of the need to preserve their sense of identity, as is the case with the American Indian and Eskimo. These tend to be the groups who lived in more fertile areas where they had time to devote to artistic endeavors such as cave paintings. And where the Aborigines are successfully employed and have some feeling of solidarity, they have banded together for social action to improve their lot. The natives of Elcho Island have their own village council and one of the consistent questions is "How can we keep this land for ourselves?" On the neighboring island of Yirrkalla, on the other hand, the younger Aborigines welcome the leasing of their land by mineral companies and the influx of whites. With a mineral boom, they reason, there will be work for them—and money for cars, motorcycles, and transistors. Even so, ties to old ways remain, and Aborigines still congregate at convenient meeting places in the bush or at settlements to perform modified versions of a remote way of life.

"We want to share with the whites," they say. "But we are not the whites. We are *yulngu*—ourselves."

5.
Desert and
Deep Jungle

AFRICAN BUSHMEN AND PYGMIES

There were no clouds over the dry land and no tall trees except for occasional baobabs thrusting up above other sparse vegetation. Here and there, what had been lakes during the rainy seasons were now completely dry or were shallow marshes. Small forests dotted the relatively flat ground, breaking the monotony of wide stretches of grass, thistles, or barren earth. Across one featureless stretch, several jeeps and trucks bumped their way forward. The vehicles were part of a scientific expedition searching for dwellers of the Kalahari Desert called Bushmen. Accompanied by native guides, an interpreter, cooks, a mechanic, and a photographer, the leaders of the expedition kept watch for the least sign of the illusive Bushmen. For weeks they had traveled the arid miles in this part of Southwest Africa, peering across dry water courses and low bushes for some hint of a Bushman's presence.

Once, Bushmen had roamed all over Africa, except for the Sahara, and they have been traced back for about fifty thousand years. Cave paintings and engravings many centuries old are believed to have been done by Bushmen. Today, they are a remnant people, confined to South Africa.

It is known that Bushmen and Hottentots lived in South Africa long before a stronger and taller people, the Bantu-speaking people came marching down from the north with their armies and witch doctors. The Bantu's path crossed that of yet another people who owned cattle. In time, the Bantu acquired droves of cattle of their own. The smaller Bushmen, without the metal spears, axes, and shields of the Bantu found themselves being pushed back ever southward. Then, with the first landing of Europeans at the Cape in 1652, the white men brought an even greater threat from the south. The whites took over the water holes and streams, destroying the animal life the Bushmen depended on, and killing the Bushmen. The Bushmen were in a vise.

White settlement was gradual but there were bloody raids against the Bushmen. Great numbers, men and women, were killed, their children carried back to white settlements as slaves. For over two hundred years, along the expanding frontier of the whites, the Bushmen were hounded and shot on sight. The Bantu, too, captured Bushmen to use as slaves. They, in turn, were victims of white slave traders who forcibly removed them from their native land and shipped them to foreign ports.

Almost all the Bushmen perished except those left in the Kalahari, a hilly and arid plateau of about 350,000 square miles in southern Bechuanaland. There, between 1800 and 1860, as the white Afrikaners exploded across the frontiers in ever increasing numbers, the Bushmen managed to survive.

Part of the technique of their survival was that they made themselves all but invisible to potential enemies. The approach of strangers made them glide back into protective cover, leaving only their footprints to give a clue to their whereabouts. The land itself was a protection, its ruggedness discouraging travelers. Even today much of it remains unexplored by outsiders.

The Bushmen are a small, handsome, agile people. Their only physical likeness to the Negro tribes living at the edge of their territory is their tightly curled, peppercorn hair. Their color is a light, reddish yellow, which becomes darker from years of sunlight. Babies are born a light pink. The Bushmen resemble the Pygmies who live in the tropical Ituri Forest in the heart of Africa, but they are taller. The Pygmies of the Ituri average a little more than four feet in height, whereas the Bushmen may measure from four feet ten inches to five feet two inches.

Like the Australian Aborigine he has learned to live in what would seem a wasteland to most people. Every source of food, whether plant or animal, is used to fill his stomach—and his stomach is often empty, especially during the long drought that begins around March and lasts until December, the hottest part of the year. June and July are the peak of the winter months, with freezing nights. The Bushman can go without food for a long while, but when he does have a chance to eat his fill, he can eat enormously and still appear as trim at the end of his feast as at the beginning. Wrinkles come with age—and in the Bushman's case this can be at twenty-five or thirty. By the time he is forty, he will be very wrinkled. He has no livestock, no permanent home, and he does no planting. He stays in one place only so long as it provides sustenance, then moves on. Hunting is for the men only—a woman may not even touch their arrows. The making of fire, also, is the men's special province. On their treks from one place to another, the Bushmen carry only the most essential items, to avoid being overburdened.

Elizabeth Marshall Thomas, who lived among the Bushmen, called them "the harmless people" in her book of that title. She found that they had a gracefulness of movement that made even the most ordinary activities such as walking or picking up something from the ground like a dance movement. Another author who ventured into the Kalahari to visit the Bushmen was Laurens Van Der Post, himself born on the rim of the Bushman country, son of Dutch parents. For him the image of the Bushman was vivid from childhood and he was fascinated by tales of the golden-skinned, Pan-eared little man who was exactly the right size, neither too large nor too small, and who was as fleet as the antelopes he pursued.

He had to be swift and strong to conquer the wild game that came within his reach at favorable seasons. He had to outwit his potential victims—ostriches, giraffe, springbok, hartebeests. Together with his marvelous tracking ability, he had concocted a lethal poison to apply to his arrowheads. The poison comes from the pupae of certain kinds of beetles which the Bushman crushes, smearing the juice on his arrows directly behind the points. He carries his arrows point down in a quiver, protecting himself from an accidental scratch or cut since a single drop entering his bloodstream would kill him within a day. For a larger creature such as a giraffe the poison works more slowly but it is equally lethal.

Not all Bushmen live in desert country. The river Bushmen live in dense, papyrus swamps of the Okovanggo River where the jungle swarms with mosquitoes and dangerous snakes. The redeeming feature is an abundance of water. In such areas, the Bushman learned how to construct intricate traps woven from reeds, with which he caught fish. And among the river reeds he dug pits, spikes carefully concealed in the center, for an unwary hippopotamus.

On the dry, vast stretches of central Bechuanaland, the Gwikwe Bushmen have no trustworthy sources of water for nine months of the year. Antelope are a main source of livelihood in the Kalahari but the hunting is difficult and usually requires long, thirsty marches. Or traps may be set. The Bushman makes snares of woven fibers in the shape of a noose laid around a pit covered with grass and branches. The end of the rope is tied to the springy stem of a nearby sapling. The stem is buried in the sand and so triggered that the lightest touch of an animal's paw or hoof will spring it. As the branch whips upright, the noose circles the animal and jerks it into the air where it hangs until the hunter kills it.

The Bushmen use almost every part of an animal they kill. The blood, along with liquid from the stomach, is a precious source of fluid. If there is more meat than the group can eat at one time, it is cut into strips and dried in the sun for future use. The hide may become a cape, a woman's loincloth apron, or fashioned into straps to carry articles. Bones are saved as hones for sharpening knives. Whoever owns the arrow that killed the animal "owns" the beast in the sense that it is his responsibility to pass around the bounty. Sharing is necessary to the survival of all, and it is done according to kinship claims or as a matter of mutual obligation.

One of the most delicious treats for the Bushman was—and is—honey. Next to his water holes and springs, his bees' nests were the most precious. He contrived to collect the honey from wild bees in such a way that the bees were not disturbed. Ownership of nests was passed on from father to son. If something happened to destroy a swarm, the Bushman would set out to find a new one, his keen eyes following the flight of a single bee even at a remote distance. If it vanished, he would note the spot, then return again and again until he had tracked the bee to its hive. In this hunt he had the help of a little, honey-loving bird who when it found a hive would streak through the air, fluttering its wings in excitement. When the Bushman found the hive, he was careful to leave the bird its share.

Traveling always in search of food, the Bushman bedded down wherever he happened to be. His bed might be nothing more than a hole scooped out in the earth, open to the sky or protected by a light brush shelter. At a semipermanent base such as a reliable water source he might build a village of tiny, dome-shaped huts made of grass and brush, called scherms. Even in these villages, the scherms are so slightly built that the wind soon blows them away. Each group of nomads has its own specific territory which it alone may use. The territory may be several hundred square miles in area but the people who claim it know every stick and stone.

Mostly, the Bushmen travel in small hunting groups composed of a few families, although in the rainy season when the land is more fruitful, larger groups may gather together for socializing. The structure of the band is loose, the members not necessarily related, and there can be a considerable drifting in and out of bands. There are no chiefs, though there are leaders and medicine men, and elders have authority by virtue of experience. There is no slavery or class distinctions, but differences in talent and temperament inevitably create varying roles for each individual.

When Elizabeth Thomas visited a band of Kung Bushmen in 1951, she discovered that most had never before seen whites other than settlers, and none had ever seen a woman born in America. They came by the dozens to sit and stare at her and her mother, once Mrs. Thomas had been able to overcome their fear and shyness. Through their contact with traders and settlers they were familiar with tobacco, which they craved and seldom had. Gifts of tobacco and salt by the Thomas group so pleased them that when a year later the expedition visited them again, they were camped in wait beside the tracks the truck had left.

What little clothing the Bushmen wear is made from the skins of animals. The man wears a leather loincloth and the woman a small, leather apron. She also may wear a leather cape, knotted at the shoulder in such a way that it forms a pouch near her hip where a baby can ride or where she can carry ostrich eggs used as water containers. A carryall, an open weave net, is an important part of her apparel.

At Bushmen camps it is common to see a row of ostrich egg shells securely placed upright in the sandy soil, their open tops plugged with grass to keep the water inside from evaporating. These ostrich shells are also used for ornaments, fragments of them made into small beads to be worn around arms and knees, or dangling in strings from tufts of hair. Mostly, the people go barefoot, though sometimes they wear leather sandals.

Although the men bring in the game meat that all Bushmen relish, the women rove miles around campsites in search of roots, seeds, wild cucumbers, and melons. Ground tsama melon seeds are a staple, roasted and ground into flour. The moist, juicy pulp of the fruit is one of the few sources of water during the dry season, aside from the blood of animals. In the hot season, the melons vanish, and then a bitter, watery root called *bi* becomes the mainstay of the Bushmen's diet.

The moon is at the center of the Bushman mythology and they do dances to it. The Kung Bushmen fear spirits of the dead, and will sing and dance to drive the spirits away. Both Kung and Gwikwe men believe that illness can be cured by exorcising evil, especially through the power of medicine men. The Bushman is secretive about his religion, and religion does not dominate his life. He has too many practical necessities to attend to, and he reserves his ceremonies or rites for the more lush seasons of the year.

Bushmen are fond of music and singing and they have several stringed instruments, but no drums. As a substitute they clap their cupped hands together or make a drumming sound on the earth by stamping it with their feet. No matter how poor or desperate, the Bushmen manage to have some musical instrument on hand. There are games, also, which include a kind of checkers played on squares marked in the sand, or a form of badminton, a buzzard's feather attached to a heavy nut to serve as a shuttlecock. They also play at war but it is truly a game.

Wherever the Bushmen are, they remain shy of whites for experience has taught many that working for white men can be an unhappy experience. Some white farmers looking for free, or nearly free, labor have exploited them, paying very little for their work, making up the rest with castoff clothing. It is against the law to keep these Aborigines against their will, but in remote regions laws are often not enforced and some Bushmen have been enslaved. The Bushmen do not trust their Bantu-speaking neighbors much more than the whites for the Bantu are even less generous, if only because they are less wealthy than the European farmers. Though the Bushmen trade with the Bantu, coming in from the veld to barter game and hides, they cling to their harsh world as safer and more desirable than the world outside.

The number of Bushmen are rapidly diminishing and with the general acquisition of modern products—whether sewing machines, safety pins, or commercially woven cloth—they are losing their native crafts. None today, for instance, creates the rock paintings that have been admired by artists and scientists. And on the edges of their territories they increasingly mingle with and vanish into the dominant white culture. The customary cry of one Bushman greeting another is "I saw you from afar!" a deliberate flattery suggesting that the other is so tall as to stand out from the landscape. How much longer that greeting will echo across the Kalahari or other Bushman territories, no one can tell. But it is not apt to be long.

In the dense shadow of huge trees festooned with fig vines and lianas, a white explorer sat waiting for a Pygmy with golden-brown skin to finish his close inspection of everything about the white stranger—his clothes, his tent, his cameras. Obviously the little man, scarcely more than four feet high, had never encountered a white man before. Yet, he was not young. There was gray in his woolly head and in the tufts of hair on his chest. Like his less daring companions who hung back in the jungle shadows, he wore only a breech clout of bark cloth. Wiry, perfectly proportioned, he would have seemed like an athletic child except for his wrinkles. His eyes shone with curiosity and even amusement. It was apparent that he was struck by the paleness of the visitor's skin. He moistened his thumb and rubbed it against the man's hand to see if the sickly pallor was real or whether it would come off.

Emboldened by the first Pygmy's daring, other Pygmies came forward to stand in a circle, grinning. Among them stood several women, so short that they, too, looked like children, their babies on their hips in a sling suspended from their shoulders. Many had manufactured glass beads around their necks and wrists, and wore a variety of ornaments in their pierced ears and through their noses—cotter pins, nails, needles, bits of flowers or grass. Some of the men, too, wore typical pieces of finery such as porcupine quills through the septums of their noses, and tiny caps of woven grass bedecked with bristles of wild pig and bright birds' feathers.

It had not been easy for the explorer to find this group of true Pygmies, the Bambuti of the Ituri Forest, for they had vanished before him as if it were true that they could not stand one whiff of the white man's smell. The odor of tobacco was another thing for they loved both pipes and cigarettes. So now, as the white visitor dispensed tobacco, the group sat around puffing vigorously, chattering to each other.

Many persons think that most African natives inhabit jungles. Actually, the majority make their homes at the edge of the jungle. Without clearing the jungle—which grows back very rapidly—agriculture is impossible. Others do not feel at home in it. The Bantu-speaking peoples shun it, disliking its gloom and shadows. The Bambuti Pygmies, however, live in the heart of the Congo forests drained by the Ituri River. Other Pygmy-like stocks live along the middle Congo River or in the eastern highlands near lakes Tanganyika and Kivu. They are larger cousins of the Bambuti called the Batwa, and are probably related to the Bushman. They, like the Bushman, use the "click" language, so called for a clicking form of enunciation.

When the Albert National Park was created in the province of Kivu, it was ordained that the Pygmies should have complete sanctuary there, free from interference. And so some of the Little People pursue their ancestral ways within its boundaries.

The majority of Pygmies, however, are increasingly in touch with the outside world if only because they have become a tourist attraction. Following the trails of Bantu, who made clearings for plantings and villages, came roads and even highways. With the highways came movie crews, news photographers, and tourists on "safari."

The Bantu-speaking people and the Pygmies have a complex and interdependent relationship. Although the Bantu adopt a disdainful attitude toward their small neighbors, explaining to white men that they are really animals, they have long obtained game from them, ivory, and also labor. In fact, the Bantu needs the Pygmy more than the Pygmy needs the Bantu. The Pygmies pretend to respect the Bantu and do their bidding, but they laugh behind their backs, secretly considering them rather dull-witted. The Bantu think that they are doing the Pygmies a great favor by trading them sugar cane, bananas, yams, tobacco, and palm wine in exchange for the game the Pygmies provide, but they are dependent on these forest people for such meats, not caring for the life of a forest hunter. They commonly refer to Pygmies as "ours," setting themselves up as masters. The Pygmies humor them, and even go through certain Bantu ceremonies—though not to the point of self-mutilation—but basically follow their own ways and beliefs. White explorers or traders depend on the Bantu to be their middlemen in association with the Little People.

All intruders, black or white, have learned to respect the Pygmies' formidable arrows. Small though these are, the poisoned arrowheads are painfully effective against man or beast. Spears and nets are also part of the Pygmies' arsenal against animals that provide them with meat and skins, and youngsters learn to hunt at an early age.

Even though the Pygmies are wanderers and plant no gardens of their own, they do build villages. Their tiny, round habitations are built of sticks, mud, and leaves, the leaves forming a canopy against the jungle rains. Whenever a new camp is made, the women usually build the huts, although men may sometimes help. Such huts are often unnoticed in the shadows of the forest. Many a traveler has gone through Pygmy territory silently escorted by Pygmy trackers without ever being aware of their presence.

Their social structure is simple, based primarily on the family. There is no hereditary chief but a skilled hunter or fighter may be accepted as a temporary leader. There are no formal councils. The degrees of specialization of tasks among men and women are comparatively minor, and women are not discriminated against as in some African societies. Women have a full and important role—even hunting is a joint effort. At the same time, a man does not feel demeaned if he picks mushrooms or has to care for a baby. If a woman has something of importance to say, she is free to speak. Children are not excluded from adult activities except from singing certain songs and the religious ritual called the *molimo*.

The *molimo* ritual is performed in times of crisis, consisting chiefly of songs sung nightly by the men. *Molimo* is also the name given to a musical instrument, a long trumpet usually made of wood, that plays an important part. The instrument delivers a mournful, singing sound, almost like a human voice, and is often used to intone a kind of answer to the men's songs. Carried around by its attendants and its musicians, it makes a haunting background for the jungle singers, sounding from one spot and then another, like a reassuring echo telling the Pygmies that all is well. To the Pygmies it is the voice of the forest itself, welding them and the forest into one being.

The origin of the Pygmies is unknown, but it is certain that they have been in central Africa far longer than the Bantu-speaking Negroes. No serious study was made of the Pygmies until the 1920s, and by then their culture had been impinged on by the Bantu.

For all that the Pygmies resist the encroachment of outside culture, they are a dwindling people. Each year more leave their old ways, either lured or pressed into modern man's culture. Nobody knows how many Pgymies there are. Of around the fifty thousand estimated to live in the Congo Basin, the greatest number seems to be in the Ituri where there may be around twenty thousand Bambuti. But the forest roads drive ever deeper. More tourists, explorers, and moving picture companies arrive —with tobacco, salt, palm wine, and money. The Little

People are overshadowed by giant neighbors, giant bull-dozers, giant threats. The discovery of gold, oil, or some other valuable resource could mean an abrupt end to what little is left of their cultural inheritance.

6.
Green Islands,
Blue Lagoons

SOUTH SEA YAPS AND MANUS

Dive bombers hurtled low over the coconut palms of the island, their shark-nosed missiles streaking toward an enemy airfield. Offshore, a massive gray warship lay at anchor, guns aimed across a blue-green lagoon. Except for tattered palms and the torn remains of thatched huts, the island seemed a most unlikely place for the thundering machines of war. Once, like hundreds of other islands in the South Seas, it had been a symbol of tranquillity, a place for romantic adventure and idle dreaming. Artists and poets had extolled the beauty of Polynesian women in Tahiti and Samoa, and the Yapese in Micronesia. Contrariwise, other visitors had reported on the cannibalism of the Fiji Islanders of the Melanesian group. And in fact there had been rigorous warfare among the islanders for centuries, more than anywhere outside Europe. Now, in the Second World War, the whole South Pacific was a battlefield, American and Australian military forces pitched against those of the Japanese entrenched among the lagoons and mountain fastnesses. Oceania, the collective name for all the islands of the South Pacific, had become a place of furious struggle, the yellow peoples and the white locked in combat while the dusky-skinned islanders were trapped in between.

Guadalcanal, the Solomon Islands, Iwo Jima—such names were to become as well known to Americans as New York or Los Angeles. In Micronesia, with some two thousand islands, the Japanese had built illegal fortifications and only after four years were they driven out. Guam, the Marianas, Bikini, these too became a part of the American vocabulary. But there were other islands where battles raged or military bases were built that remained remote and obscure to many on the home front. Yet it was in these remote places that some of the greatest cultural upheavals took place as the modern age impinged on primitive societies.

Long before World War II, the South Seas had been visited by Europeans. The Portuguese Magellan was the first to explore the East Pacific in 1520. As early as 1668 Spanish priests were busy in Micronesia, trying to convert the natives to Christianity. Adventurers, whalers, and scientists followed, roaming from island to island. Some islands were successively ruled by Spain, Germany, Japan, the United States, and Great Britain.

Typical of many of the islands in relation to

foreign rule is the Yap Island group at the western tip of the Carolines. Yap includes four islands and ten small islets circling a lagoon nineteen miles wide. First discovered by the Spanish in the 1790s, Yap was later claimed by Germany. In 1914, the Japanese seized the islands and were given a mandate over them after World War I. When in World War II the United States captured Micronesia, the area was made a trust territory of the United Nations, with the United States as the trustee.

"A Visit to a Garden of Eden," a current newspaper travel feature on Yap is headlined. Under a picture of two women, naked except for their grass skirts, the caption reads, "Some day, tourists will come and spoil it all."

Yap's native culture in the past was strongly resistant to the influences of invader and tourist. But in Yap, as elsewhere in the South Seas, the tempo of modern civilization's impact is increasingly swift. For a time, contact with the "civilized" world threatened the Yapese with extinction. The Yap population once numbered about fifty thousand. During the 1920s and 1930s it decreased to less than three thousand. The American administration is credited with saving the Yapese since the population appears to be now stabilized at around six thousand. Even so, the stresses brought about by alien visitors and technology have been so great that early Yapese culture can be said to have vanished.

An outstanding feature of the Yap society was their "money," thick stone disks, called *fei.* The stones, with holes in their centers so that they could be carried on poles, measured from six inches to a dozen feet in diameter. The larger coins were sometimes lined up like wagon wheels in the owner's yard, as impressive a symbol of wealth as a private fleet of Cadillacs today. Some belonged to an entire village instead of an individual. They were not used as currency for ordinary transactions, but were used in ceremonies and valued as symbols of prestige. The stones from which the disks were made were available only in the Palau Islands over three hundred miles away. It has happened that when men transporting the stones in a canoe encountered stormy weather, the stones were lost overboard. The spot where the stones went down was marked, and it was considered that the buyer still owned them and they remained a part of his wealth.

Although modern currency now circulates in Yap, the Yapese are reluctant to give up their stone money to outsiders. Museums are eager to procure the curious disks, and some succeed. Even though the Yapese may receive twenty-five dollars or more a diameter foot, they often regret the sale. They have seen too many periods of change in currency value. First, the Spanish money was good, then the Germans took over and the Spanish money was worthless. Next, the Japanese came and the German money lost value. After that were the Americans, and the Japanese money had no worth. Stone money, the Yaps say, remains good, even though they do not actually use it to purchase a Coke or chewing gum or the kinds of modern wares the Yapese are becoming accustomed to.

As long as the United States remains the trustee, nickels, dimes, and dollars will signify wealth instead of the moss-grown *fei* in the forests, or the encrusted disks under the sea.

About half of the inhabitants have been converted to the Roman Catholic faith. Others were converted to Shintoism or Buddhism under the Japanese. Their original religious cults are not highly organized. Ancestor worship is a common feature but there are few set rituals. Witch doctors have influence but there is no priest class. The witch doctor, called a *machamach* (magician), was at one time a very vital part of the society, working his wizardry with herbs, bones, lizard skins, and a magic wand made from the poisonous barb of the sting ray. The *machamach* supposedly could ensure good weather by blowing into a conch shell or put a curse on anyone he wished. Today, young men who might have accepted training to become *machamachs* are educated away from such training. So, most of the remaining witch doctors find themselves without heirs.

The Yapese are small of stature, with medium brown skin and wavy hair, and their origins are little known. On their volcanic islands, the coconut is paramount as a source of food and drink, and its shells, fronds, and fibers have many uses. Grated coconut meat is an important item of trade, and the sun-dried meat called copra is an ingredient of fine soaps. Fishing is the chief activity of the men, often taking place at night by torchlight. The fishermen fish in conventional ways, but also use poison to kill fish that have been herded into cave pools or shallow lagoons. During the fishing season the men are forbidden to stay in their own houses and must assemble at the community bachelor house. This long, narrow house is built by young men and they must remain there until they marry.

Coconut palms form the steeply slanting roofs of the typical Yap house. Once these houses were situated according to warring tribes, but now little attention is paid to boundaries that once separated hostile groups. In earlier days, men were heavily tattooed. The women were not, with the exception of a special mistress assigned to the bachelor house. Except for their long grass skirts, the women wear only ornaments in their hair or around their necks. Equally simple are the men's loincloths, seminakedness being natural in a climate that is hot and humid.

During the war Yap was devastated both by Allied bombers and Japanese defenders. The latter destroyed hundreds of native houses because they needed wood and thatch as fuel. They broke up the Yaps' stone money to use the crushed rock for road surfacing, as Germans had done before them. From over thirteen thousand pieces of such money counted in 1929, only six thousand remained after the war. Yapese men were forced to work on airfields or in mines, without pay. Soldiers helped themselves to whatever struck their fancy, including Yapese women.

Although the Japanese are long gone, their Zeros still lie rotting alongside air strips or in the jungle. Near them rain-filled bomb craters glisten. In many places, live artillery ammunition, grenades, and land mines remain in the ground, making the land dangerous for any but demolition experts. Bombs destroyed many coconut plantations, and subsequent neglect brought about a lowering in the quality of the nuts, though this is being remedied. Yapese men dislike farming, for it is not a part of their background. When farming is a basis of life, men do it. Otherwise, it is women's work. Most of the roads built during Japanese occupation have deteriorated or been overgrown by the jungle. Many bridges destroyed in the war have still not been restored. Villagers travel chiefly on foot or by boat, and the journey to market may be so long that their farm or garden produce spoils on the way. Children who live far from school go untaught. The sick or injured in isolated villages often die before they can be brought to a hospital, although American administrators have done much to improve health conditions. All known lepers have been isolated, and the tropical disease called yaws is said to have been eradicated.

Travel agents are fond of proclaiming that Yap is one of the places in the world left "unspoiled." Nevertheless, the ancient ways have been uprooted. It is becoming commonplace for native women to cluster around a newly arrived airliner, offering to put on a native dance for a stated fee. After all, it is not easy to buy tickets to the movies in the main city of Colonia, or TV dinners at the supermarket, with stone "money" or by barter.

Up until around 1965, private automobiles or

motor scooters were practically unknown in the islands. Three years later there were two hundred and fifty scooters buzzing over the roads and trails, and one hundred rattling jalopies. In the past, people seldom ventured far beyond their own particular villages. Now, with friends and relatives scattered, those who can afford it, use the gasoline engine to race from one end of the main island to the other—all of sixteen miles. The law requires the rider of a motor scooter to wear a crash helmet. Since there are few helmets to be had, or the rider lacks money for one, the Yapese go racing past with pots and pans strapped to their heads.

The goal of the United States' trusteeship is to help Yap and other Micronesian islands to become self-governing and self-sufficient. Neither in Yap nor the other islands is this happening very swiftly. Part of the problem is lack of a sound economic base and long-range planning. According to Hawaiian Representative Patsy T. Mink, returning from the islands in 1970, there has been appalling mismanagement and neglect, with burgeoning needs among the natives that challenge the best efforts of teachers, doctors, and technologists. Though the United States has been the trustee since 1947, it long had difficulty deciding what policy to pursue. Up until 1965, the "zoo" theory was followed, in which the islanders were to be left alone and "unspoiled." The "spoiling" had already taken place with the extreme disruption of native cultures by the war and exposure to alien ways.

The emphasis now is on developing the territory

economically and encouraging Micronesians toward a sense of unity and nationhood. To this end, the United States authorized a Micronesian bicameral Congress—one having two legislative chambers. But the task of uniting diverse groups is a complex one. Only ninety-six of the 2100 islands are inhabited, for a total overall population of around 97,000. Nine different languages are spoken, and whereas some islands are technologically advancing others remain at a primitive level. However, according to the High Commissioner, Edward Johnston, nearly 90 per cent of elementary age children are in school, and the enrollment of children in secondary school is up from 295 in 1955 to 3700 in 1969.

What the ultimate status of Micronesia will be is uncertain. Some United States senators have spoken of the possibility of ultimately annexing Micronesia to Hawaii, along with other Pacific Islands, under United States trusteeship, as one great Pacific state—if the islanders desired this. In actual practice, dominant powers pay little attention to the wishes of unequal ones, so perhaps the Yapese and other islanders will have not much more to say about their future than the Hawaiians did or the American Indian.

One of the most interesting outgrowths of culture contact in the South Pacific was the development of a nativistic cult called the Cargo Cult. The cult spread throughout the South Pacific, taking different forms in different areas, but the governing idea was essentially the same. Economics in the form of material goods was at its base, but its superstructure was one including ritual and myth. Impressed by the products, tools, and machines of the outside technological world, certain natives were seized by the belief that these goods could become theirs automatically, out of the very strength of their desire, particularly if they destroyed the possessions they already owned. The cult infected whole groups so that entire villages tossed their possessions and even their food into the sea, then waited for the Western world's cargo to appear.

The cult flourished to new heights as a result of the island invasions during World War II. Having seen the mountains of materials delivered by military troop ships, and recognizing their value, the islanders became imbued with the belief that some day such cargo would be theirs alone. The goods would arrive, one way or another. Perhaps a great cargo ship would sail to them, bringing everything from automobiles to air conditioners, and the ingenious machines where all one had to do was to push a button to get food, candy, or cigarettes. Why work at getting food if all that one had to do was to push a button? Chosen sentinels watched for days and nights for the arrival of the ships or planes that would deliver goods for the natives alone.

When such cargo did not arrive as expected, the islanders watched the white men more closely, trying to discover the source of their power over cargo. They saw how the whites erected tall masts with long wires attached, and how they then sat listening to the curious boxes that gave out beeping or squawking noises or even the sound of human voices. And they watched soldiers marching in drill. Neither the radio towers nor the drilling of troops made any sense to them except that they appeared to be magic structures and rituals that brought the cargo. So they built their own imitation towers out of wood and vines. They acquired scraps of military uniforms, carved harmless rifles out of wood, and tried to march up and down the way the soldiers did. Some constructed crude, full-size copies of airplanes which they placed on hilltops, guarded by native "pilots."

Leaders and self-appointed prophets rose among the various peoples, some exploiting the Cargo Cult expectations toward their own ends. In the highlands of New Guinea, one "prophet" claimed that a fleet of shining planes would arrive in the valley. The natives built large storehouses to assure the cargo deities that they were prepared to take good care of the riches they hoped to receive. Another group believed that a tunnel would open up in a mountainside and lines of trucks, loaded with gifts, would rumble forth. Priests of the new faith stirred their audiences into a frenzy of expectation. In still another group, the cult was especially intense, the leaders prophesying that the white world would collapse entirely and all its treasures be shipped to the island.

The Americans unwittingly contributed to the Cargo Cult movement. During the war, soldiers gave away everything they did not need at the moment—surplus food, clothing, radios, tools, even partly worn-out machines. And at the end of the war, tons of equipment were left where they stood on the conquered beaches. Then the soldiers departed, leaving it all to the first takers. The islanders were left to dream that it would happen again, on an even bigger scale. Well after the war, the cult maintained its strength and even increased. In the Solomons, New Britain, and New Guinea, the idea spread that the cargo would be personally delivered by a fleet under the personal command of President Lyndon B. Johnson. In New Guinea, in local elections, people were told to vote for whomever they preferred as their head chief. They voted for President Johnson.

Off the coast of New Guinea lie the Admiralty Islands. Perhaps no islanders were more dramatically affected by the presence of American troops than these, for it was here that the United States established one of the largest military bases between Pearl Harbor and Guam. The thirteen or fourteen thousand inhabitants of the Admiralties had been exposed to foreign influence before. At the time the Japanese invaders arrived, they were under the dominion of Australia. The small force of Australian administrators evacuated quickly before the far superior might of the Japanese. On the main island of Manus, the Japanese settled down to exploit the natives, conscripting them for labor under military law, and enforcing their will. It was a period of fear and suffering for the Manus. When the first wave of American fighter planes zoomed down to strike at the Japanese outpost in

Peri village on Manus, the people remembered how the Japanese had assured them that such planes would not come. So, the Japanese had lied. The Manus islanders fled to swamps and caves. They came out only after American forces had landed and went among them with an Australian interpreter, reassuring them and enlisting their help in routing the Japanese from other hiding places.

More and more American soldiers arrived, reportedly as many as a million before the war was over. They were of every type and kind—white, black, yellow, brown—and with them they brought masses of machinery and goods. The primitive Manus were fascinated by the power of those machines, the bulldozers clearing air strips, caterpillars snorting up steel hills, chain saws gnawing into trees and brush, steam shovels biting off chunks of mountains to flatten them into landing fields. Further, the Americans were friendly and good-humored, far different from most other foreigners who had come among them. The Americans treated the half-naked, frizzy-haired, dark-skinned Manus as fellow human beings, and generously shared their food, gum, cigarettes, or other treats. And many of the soldiers were as dark skinned as themselves.

Thanks to anthropologist Margaret Mead, it is possible to know what the Manus islanders were like when the American Army arrived in 1942, and even earlier when Dr. Mead visited the island in 1928. It was as a result of her first visit that she wrote her famous book *Growing Up in New Guinea*. In 1928, she found about two thousand half-naked "savages" living in pile dwellings in salt lagoons offshore. People, including small children, glided about in boats, or swam as if they were half fish. Ear lobes were laden with shells, the men's hair fashioned into great knots or combed up in a high friz ornamented with red combs. Bristling dog's teeth collars were considered high fashion for women on feast days, or decorative strands of shell money. A bride was dressed and ornamented in an especially extravagant fashion at her wedding. Her kinky black hair was dyed red, while her face, arms, and back were painted orange. Girdles and bands of dog's teeth were arranged on her forehead, arms, and breasts. A kind of girdle of the teeth supported two heavy shell aprons, and tucked into her arm bands were such foreign-made articles as knives, mirrors, or forks and spoons.

To a stranger watching the large, outrigger canoes move gracefully between the stilt-legged houses that were perfectly designed to withstand gusts of wind or wave, and hearing laughter or shouts from certain canoes, the Manus seemed to live an idyllic life. But they were ghost haunted, and nearly every activity was governed by rigid laws. Only certain relatives were permitted to laugh together. As for ghosts, each house had its own internal shrine to a departed ancestor, often the spirit of the most recently dead male. Though the articles the natives used—handsome baskets, soup ladles with intricately carved handles, ornate lime sticks to be rattled against delicately incised lime gourds, tassels of shell money—indicated high artistic ability, none was made by the Manus themselves but were obtained by trade with peoples outside. The Manus did not even have the necessary materials to work with; even the logs they used for house posts had to be imported. Lacking almost everything in the way of natural resources except fish and shell fish, their skills were mainly those of navigators and boatbuilders. The advantage of their watery location was that they felt safe from attacks from the land people. By clever bargaining and hard labor at fishing, they managed to be supplied with what they needed, and felt both rich and proud.

Typical Manus were those who lived in the village of Peri on the southeast coast, and it was on these that Dr. Mead focused her book *New Lives for Old*. In spite of exposure to white men's ways, the Manus remained faithful to, and driven by, their complex rituals and traditions. Property of any kind, so laboriously obtained by trips to various islands, was highly valued, and they had a keen practical sense. The economic system was elaborate, governing the lives of everyone in the community, as with us. Money was dog's teeth and shell beads and, after tobacco was introduced, tobacco sticks. The value of all goods was accurately measured: so many dog's teeth for a container of oil, a comb, or a supply of betel nuts, which all natives chewed with pleasure. The dog teeth and shell currency played a very important economic part in marriages, as well.

The elders decided who should marry whom,

choosing future partners while these were still children although unwilling partners could often find ways to circumvent this. Once married, the loyalty of the husband was to his own clan, that of the wife to hers, instead of to each other. The young bridegroom was financed by interested backers, men who acted like a modern loan company. Consequently, he was placed in debt and was required to work exclusively for the donor who might be an uncle or an elder cousin. Although a hard-working young man could pay off his debt in a relatively short time, not all were so successful, and the system contributed to what Dr. Mead calls "an economic treadmill."

Dominated by ancestral spirits, driven to harvest the sea in exchange for goods from the land dwellers, unfamiliar with any world but their own, the Manus at the time of the landing of the American armies were a startling contrast to what they are today. In the comparatively short time between the coming of the Americans and a return visit by Dr. Mead in 1953, the Manus had almost literally leaped into the new world. They had moved their houses out of the sea, adopted Western-style clothes, set up democratic voting procedures, and were zealously building schools, clinics, churches, and cooperatives, dedicated to what they called the New Way.

This new era began in 1946, but there were beginnings of the change before the arrival of the American troops. In the thirties, when most of the people became converted to Catholicism, the Manus dethroned their household ghosts. Many young men who had been sent to school outside their villages, or had worked under white administrators, returned to their homes urging that a modernized system be set up to replace the old ways. One of these young men was called Paliau. He was not a Manus but a native of the tiny island of Baluan. Having served as a young police recruit under the Australians, he returned to his home island with many resentments against the rigid patterns of the old life. This was before the Japanese invasion. Then the Japanese came, and after them the Americans. Property minded as the Manus were, they were fascinated by American material riches. And American expressions of the idea of a common brotherhood stimulated the common man's imagination, as well as that of such native leaders as Paliau.

After the war, the Admiralty Islands returned to the administration of Australia. The Australians, not nearly so rich in goods as the profligate Americans, found the Manus "spoiled" in their expectation of material things. Returned work boys were discontent and sullen. Each of the eleven Manus villages had special targets of discontent—the dominance of the older men, use of old-fashioned dog's teeth money, the native costumes, the taboos relating to kinship. Paliau was a leader for the discontented and outlined a complete break with the old way of life, which then included a hodgepodge mixture of primitive beliefs and Christianity. He pictured a society that would resemble European and American, but his ideas for bringing this about were vague. However, he continued to gather together supporters, chiefly among the Manus, the strongest group in the area.

People in the various islands began preparing for the new way of life, and on one of the islands the Cargo Cult exploded into fresh frenzy. Hysterical prophets told of the coming of ships and planes with the white man's goods. The frenzy spread to the Manus of Peri village. A messenger brought the news that the cargo had already arrived in ships anchored off a specified shore. These ships, the woman messenger said, wanted to come to Peri but were blocked because of all the antique possessions the people clung to. Such possessions, she declared, were like a reef preventing the ships from entering the waters of Peri. Everything must be thrown away before the new cargo would arrive.

And so the Cargo Cult movement called "The Noise" came to Peri. Obsessed with the belief that they must make way for the wonderful goods of the modern world, the natives seized their belongings—shell money, baskets, pottery, dancing spears, ornaments—and tossed them into the lagoon until the water was choked with property. After the sacrifice, the people sat waiting in their empty houses and in the Catholic church. Days passed and no cargo came. Disillusioned, at last, angry, the people rejected the false prophets and turned toward the leaders who preached the need for realistic reform in which individual effort and community responsibility were the ways to gain the good things of white civilization. This was the New Way.

It was then that the Manus began radically re-organizing their society. Old Peri of the lagoon became New Peri on shore. Ancient taboos against in-laws or prospective bride and groom talking to each other were abolished. Laughter was no longer confined to specific relatives. Why not, the people decided, let all family members have friendly times together, or let husbands and wives display affection toward each other as characters in American films did? One of the things they most favored was the adoption of a modern calendar, and this they achieved in 1946.

Dr. Mead made a third visit to Manus in 1964. In New Peri she found a large school. Teaching in English had begun ten years before, and about three dozen children had gone elsewhere to further their education. Education was not for the children alone but for the whole village. Once isolated in their lagoon houses, the people reached out and identified with those of Papua-New Guinea. Young Australian teachers were there, volunteers after a year's special training, to bring new knowledge to the ambitious Manus. All that remained of Old Peri were some house posts thrusting up above the water. In the new village, houses built according to an identical plan, stood in neat rows. There was an immaculately swept square in the center, a church hovering over all. A few of the old and sick or "backward" still clung to sea houses offshore, but the rest of the Manus were rooted in the land and a new soil.

Young persons now decide whom they will

marry, and they seek the education and occupations that will make them more a part of the modern world. Most have learned to speak a kind of pidgin English, now called Neo-Melanesian. Since no culture changes completely in a day or even a generation, some ancient habits and attitudes cling stubbornly, but the future points to democracy, literacy, and reason.

In most cases, primitive societies have vanished completely under the dominance of foreign conquerors, or have been assimilated to the point that their original way of life is obliterated. Usually, such assimilation, or even extermination, takes a long while. The Manus appear to be unique in their ability to leap the culture chasm so swiftly, but the circumstances were special. With their strong sense of property rights and their pragmatism, they were preadapted to the change. The old, abandoned ways are like the rotting house posts in the lagoons. Whether the New Way will be deeply rewarding or not depends not only on the Manus and the other peoples of New Guinea, but on the entire pattern of modern civilization with its threat of atomic or biological warfare and its problems of overpopulation, racial strife, and pollution of the natural environment.

One group of South Sea islanders became well acquainted with the menace in modern civilization's atomic bombs. Natives of Bikini in the Marshall Islands, were removed from their western Pacific atoll before the testing of nuclear bombs began there in 1946. From then until 1958, twenty-three nuclear bombs were exploded by the United States over, on, and under the atoll or its lagoon and surrounding waters. Not until 1968 did the Atomic Energy Commission decide that it was safe for the Bikinians to return. For the intervening twenty-two years, the islanders suffered terribly in trying to adapt to new conditions and new terrain so unlike what they had formerly known. The few who survived yearn to return. Though they can now return, they will find that much has changed. The Commission has determined that radiation levels do not offer a significant threat to human health, but precautions have to be observed. The Bikini atoll complex contains thirty-six islands, and those with the lowest contamination levels are to be resettled first. Even there, periodic surveys of radiation levels must be made. If the residents plant fruit-bearing Pandanus trees, two inches of topsoil should be removed first. The number of land crabs taken, a part of the normal diet in the western Pacific islands, must be reduced sharply because of their high content of strontium 90. All plant and animal life suffered from radiation damage, and there is a question in the minds of some investigators whether Bikini can ever be restored to anything like its former state.

The once uncharted and largely ignored Pacific islands represent today's new frontiers. Only in a few isolated places are there any peoples who remain beyond the noise of the machine or the clank of coins, and even there the airplane whooshes over, the shadow of its wings bearing the shape of the future.

7.
Amazon
and
Arctic

SOUTH AMERICAN INDIANS, LAPPS, AND AINUS

One of the last outposts of "wild" Indian tribes is in South America, particularly in the Amazon River basin, the tributaries of the Orinoco River in eastern Colombia and Venezuela, in parts of Paraguay and eastern Brazil, and on the slopes of the Andes in Peru and Ecuador. Depending on their location, some tribes live by farming in the tropical forests, some are nomadic fishermen, hunters, and food gatherers. Only a small percentage pursue ancient ways untouched by contact with missionaries, planters or mine operators. Such contacts, as with whites who desire their lands, have been often brutal and resulted in the extermination of uncounted numbers of Indian tribes.

Brutality is not confined to the past. In 1968, the shocking news leaked out that a systematic program of killing the forest Indians of Brazil had been undertaken by settlers. Pressed for the facts, the Brazilian Government admitted that the Indian tribes of the Amazon Basin had been virtually exterminated, not in spite of the efforts of the Indian Protection Service but sometimes with its co-operation. For twenty years, corrupt members of the Service, subservient to the greed of settlers, had been annihilating Indian tribes for their lands. The tribes were attacked from the air, dynamite dropped on them and their villages. Some tribes were given liquor to make them drunk, then shot down by gunners hired by landowners. Others were mowed down by machine guns. Two tribes were exterminated by giving them smallpox injections; others were given food containing arsenic. One investigator for the federal police found that hundreds of Indians were enslaved by plantation owners and that concentration camps were set up for lepers where they awaited death without care of any kind.

Brazil's Indian Protective Service was founded in 1911 to halt the destruction of Indian communities and values. For a time, the Indians' interests were closely guarded by the Service. But the greed of whites for these Aborigines' land—for rubber plantations, minerals, and oil—resulted in constant encroachment and a weakening of will among harassed and self-seeking agents who joined in unbelievable crimes against natives armed only with stone axes and arrows. When the truth came to light, hundreds of agents were reportedly arrested or dismissed, and a new National Indian Foundation was established. Some investigators have questioned whether the guilty were actually punished, or if any new policy will really prevent continuing genocide. Whatever the truth, protection policies of any kind are far too late for the vanished Cintas Largas Indians, the Macacalis, the Patachos, and all the others who perished in the path of conquering Europeans, as it is too late for many North American tribes who also suffered not only from soldiers and settlers but from Indian agents who were supposed to help them.

Long before the present century, the Spanish Conquistadores slaughtered thousands of the various South American Indians who stood in their way. Bartolomé de Las Casas, an early religious leader of the Dominican order, fought courageously in the Indians' behalf. The Spanish Court itself took measures to try to protect the natives, but the efforts of government, however well meaning—whether Spanish, English, or American —have seldom succeeded in enforcing brotherhood or even tolerance on those who have the power to exploit or destroy primitive peoples.

The majority of Indians in South America today are *mestizos,* those who have intermingled with the whites. Though they have lost their distinctive Indian ways they have not been thoroughly assimilated into the dominant, white Hispanic patterns. Many are artisans, laborers, or peasant farmers.

Among the wild tribes still extant, though dwindling, are the Jivaros living deep in the Amazon rain forests still unpenetrated by the white man. A vital part of their culture is the taking of human heads, not out of savagery but because long tradition demands that this is necessary. In order for a young man to survive, he must take the head of another man—usually of a relative—so that the soul of the other can enter his own body. Otherwise, lacking a soul, he is doomed to die, and that soul must be "locked into" himself. The victim's head is shrunken by an elaborate process so that its avenging soul is forced out, its power flowing into the victor and the land. Even so, the original owner's spirit grows lonely in a few years and threatens to return, so the warrior must take a new head as his "life insurance." Since the Jivaros do not want the old heads around, they trade them off. For all that the white man expressed horror at such a practice, the shrunken heads were a popular trade item in the international market for years. Even after the trade was made illegal, "civilized" buyers sought them, but the supply dwindled with the dwindling head-hunters so that purchasers often found themselves paying out hard money for what were actually shriveled monkey heads—the monkey heads also having a ritual significance in the Jivaro culture.

The Jivaros, like other South American natives, are disappearing. Many were killed by Ecuadorian and Peruvian armies during the late 1930s and early 1940s. They were considered fair game for hunting parties, remindful of white men's scalping raids in the United States in the nineteenth century. And as the white population increases throughout the coastal and upland regions of Ecuador and Peru, the Jivaros, like the Indians in other areas, are pushed back from their lands and diminished by contact with new diseases. The once proud Incas of the highlands of Peru and Bolivia are now among the poorest people in the world.

The Indians of Mexico today are of roughly two groups. There are those who subsist from the soil in rural areas, still using their short-handled hoes, wearing rain capes made of thatch, plodding behind a plow powered by an ox, their naked feet encased in leather sandals reinforced by soles cut from rubber tire casings. This is the Indian popular among photograph-taking tourists. Another group of Indians has managed to work its way into modern Mexican society, through luck or pluck, becoming everything from clerks to professionals to legislators. These "modernized" Indians are generally contemptuous of their blood brothers who have lagged behind, calling them *Indios.* Wearing modern dress, living in cities, speaking Spanish, these acculturated Indians refer to themselves as true *Mejicanos.* But there are those who, though they may be social workers, dentists, or artists, do not forswear their Indian heritage, well knowing all that the *Indios,* including the great Indian leader Benito Juárez, have contributed. In numerous Latin American countries an Indianist movement has spread so that there is an increasing national interest in the Indian past and in the welfare of Indian tribes that still exist. However, such movements grow up only where there were formerly powerful native cultures, as in Mexico where Indian motifs are strongly represented in the arts and crafts.

Quite separate from the vanishing natives of South America are the Lapps of Europe. Short of stature, with somewhat yellowish skin and dark hair, they have blue to brown eyes. Due to what is called an epicanthic or "Mongoloid" fold of their eyelids, their eyes appear slanted.

The land of the Lapps has no fixed boundaries; it extends across arctic Sweden, Norway, and Finland into Russia. Archeologists state that Lapps existed in these regions in A.D. 400. Little is known of their early history but it is believed that they came from central Asia and were pushed northward by migrations of Finns, Goths, and Slavs. Domesticated reindeer have long been the base of the Laplander's economy, providing meat, milk, and clothing, excepting those Lapps who live by the sea or rivers. As reindeer range widely in their search for moss and lichen to feed upon, the Lapp herders must follow them. "Lapp" is the Swedish word for nomad.

Relatively few of the some thirty-two thousand Lapps today follow the ancient herdsman's life which involved hauling his household supplies on a wooden sled and setting up camp wherever the reindeer paused. The younger people enter the army, migrate to the cities for jobs, or even find their way into the universities. Those who do cling to the old ways continue toiling behind their herds through an arctic landscape where it is always light in summer, always dark in winter. Like other cold-weather peoples, the Lapps have developed ingenious ways to protect themselves from sub-zero temperatures, from their deerskin boots packed with a native grass, to heavy boots curled up at the tips in order to fit into the single leather strap Lapps use on their skis. Traditional festive dress is extremely colorful, with emphasis on red. A few youngsters are still snugly strapped into a carry cradle similar to those of American Indians.

The Lapp background retains elements of ancient ritual such as offerings to the poor or crippled made by Lapps in order to bring good luck in hunting. In eating reindeer, a strict pattern is followed. Generally, the Lapp religion today is a combination of Greek Orthodox beliefs, adapted from the Russians, and Swedish Lutheranism.

Even today's Lapps, who still depend on reindeer herds for their subsistence, take advantage of mechanized vehicles such as snowmobiles to round up strays or transport supplies. Automobiles and trucks speed across the countryside, and tourists come with them. Still when the wind slaps their villages or sleds, some Lapps murmur that perhaps the "wind man is angry." Others cherish ancient songs in the face of the young people gathered around a village juke box. Soon the songs will be forgotten, and the wind man as silent as reindeer tracks disappearing into the wilderness with no herder to follow.

Japan, too, has its Aborigines, called the Ainu. These are a short, stocky people with brown eyes (lacking the epicanthic fold), wavy hair, and pale yellow complexions. The long hair of the women and the magnificent long beards of the men, together with body hair, have given them the name of the Hairy Ainu. They are settled mainly in northern Japan, on the second largest Japanese island, Hokkaido. They have a long history of war and defeat at the hands of the Japanese. Anthropologists tend to believe the Ainus are a separate race, a surviving remnant of people who lived on Hokkaido as long as seven thousand years ago. It is on this harsh, wintry island, about the size of Ireland, that the surviving Ainus remain, numbering around only three hundred. The extent of the original aboriginal population is unknown. Thousands of others are mixed bloods who have intermarried with their ancient enemy, the Japanese.

For centuries, the Ainus depended on fishing and hunting for their needs until Japanese settlers moved onto the island and changed the economy to agriculture. Before then, the sight of bearded fishermen in colorful cloth robes, covered with designs closely resembling those of the American Indians of the Northwest coast, was common. Today, both the robes and the long dugout fishing canoes are rare. Most of the Ainu settlements are close to the sea and are now in steady contact with other civilizations. What little remains of Ainu culture is preserved mainly by inland hunters. A few small villages have deliberately kept and even elaborated on what they remember from old times, trying to appeal to tourists.

The religion of the ancients was filled with a belief in invisible spiritual beings called *kamui* who lived in another world and occasionally visited the earth disguised as animals. One of the supremely important spirits was Abe-fuji-kamui, the spirit of fire, fire being extremely essential on an island of deep snows and freezing temperatures. The keeping of the fires was the women's responsibility, as it still is where modern stoves do not exist. Only the oldest women still wear broad, blue tattoos, like a second pair of lips, around their mouths. Such tattooing was prohibited by the Japanese. Young Ainus are embarrassed by a grandmother who wears such an indelible design. Only the elders have any deep regard for the old customs and they carry them on as best they can, knowing that most will disappear with them—the sacred prayer sticks, the infant cradles suspended from the ceiling, the stately crane dance in which women with fluttering shawls imitated the fluttering flight of the crane. A most important feature in the ancient religion was the Bear Cult. Ainu legends recall that once a giant bear came from his realm in the sky to rescue the people from famine. Every spring the Ainu performed a ceremony in which the bear was ritualistically killed in order to return the animal's spirit to the sky, laden with gifts and honors. Today, the festival is in a mock, attenuated form performed for curious visitors. Bears are not killed in these performances; few bears are to be found.

The Ainu language, unwritten except as its sounds

are transposed into the Japanese tongue, is rapidly disappearing. But many place names in Japan are Ainu terms such as the volcano Fujiyama, which means fire goddess. From the end of the nineteenth century onward, the Ainus have come more and more under the influence of the Japanese for it was in 1899 that the Japanese Government took over Hokkaido. Under the Native Protection Law, the Japanese gave tools to the Ainus and encouraged them to engage in agriculture. Legislation also required Ainu children to attend school and to study Japanese customs, history, and language. In 1937, compulsory classroom integration began. When World War II came, Japanese and Ainu soldiers fought side by side. Today the Ainus and Japanese work and play together, and it is the Ainus who are being absorbed. Soon the last true Ainu will be gone and anthropologists may still wonder where the original ancestors of the handsome, long-haired tribe came from.

The origins of the many various peoples on earth cannot be completely known, and obscure tribes vanished before there was such a science as anthropology. The future of present primitive or semiprimitive tribes and cultures is reasonably certain—they will disappear, swallowed up by dominant neighbors or intruders, as has happened in the past. In spite of the efforts of outsiders or the peoples themselves to preserve and perpetuate characteristic native customs and arts, it is not likely that the Eskimo's dog sled will long survive the snowmobile, or the Amazon Indians' poisoned arrows prove effective against machine guns. The Bushman, the Australian Aborigine, the Yap and the Tlingit, all are people living in a twilight zone, a period of transition between darkness and light or between light and darkness.

Most, if not all, aboriginal cultures are entering a period of sunset insofar as their old ways are concerned, and much of value will be lost with them—the marvelous tracking ability of the First Australians, the genius of the Eskimo in surviving in an ice-bound land, the reverence for nature of the American Indian, the ingenious and often masterful ways of all the diverse groups coping with equally diverse climates and soils, and their complex social and spiritual organizations.

There is no going back. The new, dominant cultures, whether in Asia, Africa, or America, are machine dominated, and technology (both good and bad) governs us all, in factory, on campus, in our homes, or in space. An ordinary respect for all mankind, not to mention the extra responsibility (and guilt) the dominant cultures share in having destroyed or corrupted earlier cultures, demands that some dignified transition from the old to the new be made possible for the dispossessed. For those groups who feel strongly bound to earlier ways, there should be as little interference as possible, or assistance if asked. For those who wish to adapt to and become a functioning part of the dominant society, there should be greatly increased opportunities to make this possible. Above all, there should be an appreciation and respect for all creative forms of human life.

A desire for well-being, individual dignity, and identity is universal, as expressed by the Australian Aborigines. "We want to share with the whites—but we are not whites. We are *yulngu*—ourselves."

Books for Further Reading

The Desperate People (Eskimos of northwestern Canada),
Farley Mowat. Little Brown & Co., 1959.

Disinherited: The Lost Birthright of the American Indian,
Dale Van Every. William Morrow & Co., 1961.

The Forest People: A Study of the Pygmies of the Congo,
Colin M. Turnbull. Simon & Schuster, 1961; Doubleday
Anchor Book, 1962.

The Islands (Hawaii), Storrs Lee. Henry Holt & Co.,
1966.

Moonlight at Midday (Alaskan Eskimos), Sally Car-
righar. Alfred A. Knopf, Inc., 1958.

Navahos Have Five Fingers, T. D. Allen. University of
Oklahoma, 1963.

*New Lives for Old: Cultural Transformation, the Manus
1928–1953,* Margaret Mead. William Morrow & Co.,
1953, 1966.

*The Passing of the Aborigines: A Lifetime Spent Among
the Natives of Australia,* Daisy Bates. John Murray,
London, 1938, 1966.

*The Patriot Chiefs: A Chronicle of American Indian
Resistance,* Alvin M. Josephy, Jr. The Viking Press,
1958; Viking Compass Book, 1961.

The Savage and the Innocent (Primitive tribes of Brazil), David Maybury-Lewis. World Publishing Co., 1965.

Vanishing Peoples of the Earth, National Geographic, 1968.

Vanishing Tribes, Roy Pinney. Thomas Y. Crowell Co., 1968.

ABOUT THE AUTHOR

Adrien Stoutenburg is a full-time writer with a varied list of books to her credit, including short stories, poetry, fiction, and non-fiction. Writing primarily in the juvenile field since 1951, she is co-author with Laura Nelson Baker of seven biographies, most recently *Listen America: A Life of Walt Whitman,* and author of two books about conservation, *A Vanishing Thunder: Extinct and Threatened American Birds* and *Animals at Bay: Rare and Rescued American Wildlife.*

A native of Minnesota, Miss Stoutenburg now lives in Lagunitas, Marin County, California.

INDEX

M

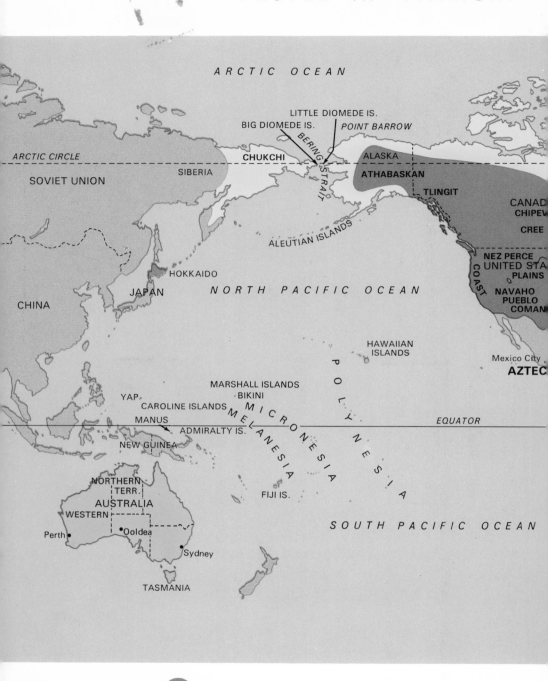

ARCTIC OCEAN

LITTLE DIOMEDE IS.
BIG DIOMEDE IS.   *POINT BARROW*

ARCTIC CIRCLE   **CHUKCHI**   **ALASKA**

SOVIET UNION   SIBERIA   **ATHABASKAN**

    TLINGIT

   CANAD
   CHIPEW
   CREE

ALEUTIAN ISLANDS

HOKKAIDO   *NORTH PACIFIC OCEAN*   **NEZ PERCE**
UNITED STA
PLAINS

CHINA   JAPAN   **NAVAHO**
PUEBLO
COMAN

HAWAIIAN
ISLANDS

Mexico City
AZTEC

MARSHALL ISLANDS
BIKINI   P O L Y N E S I A

YAP   M I C R O N E S I A
CAROLINE ISLANDS
MANUS   EQUATOR
ADMIRALTY IS.
NEW GUINEA   M E L A N E S I A

NORTHERN
TERR.
AUSTRALIA
WESTERN   FIJI IS.   *SOUTH PACIFIC OCEAN*

Perth   •Ooldea

•Sydney

TASMANIA

ARCTIC OCEAN — BERING STRAIT — COAST

● North American Indians (original scope)

● South American Indians today

● Eskimos and Aleuts

● African Bushman